ACCIDENTAL MAGIC

THE WIZARD'S TECHNIQUES FOR WRITING WORDS WORTH 1,000 PICTURES

Other books by Roy H. Williams

*The Wizard of Ads: Turning Words into Magic
and Dreamers into Millionaires*

Secret Formulas of the Wizard of Ads

*Magical Worlds of the Wizard of Ads:
Tools and Techniques for Profitable Persuasion*
(The companion book to *Accidental Magic*)

ACCIDENTAL MAGIC

THE WIZARD'S TECHNIQUES FOR WRITING WORDS WORTH 1,000 PICTURES

ROY H. WILLIAMS,
JANET THOMAE,
CHRIS MADDOCK
&
ONE HUNDRED AND SIX
GRADUATES OF
WIZARD ACADEMY

Bard Press

Austin · Atlanta

ACCIDENTAL MAGIC
THE WIZARD'S TECHNIQUES FOR WRITING WORDS WORTH 1,000 PICTURES

Roy H. Williams, Janet Thomae, Chris Maddock & One Hundred and Six Graduates of Wizard Academy

Bard Press
An imprint of Longstreet Press
2974 Hardman Court
Atlanta, GA 30305
1-800-927-1488 phone
www.bardpress.com

To order the book, contact your local bookstore or call 800-945-3132.

ISBN 1-885167-54-7 hardcover

Library of Congress Cataloging-in-Publication Data
Williams, Roy H.
  Accidental magic : the Wizard's techniques for writing words
  worth 1,000 pictures / Roy H. Williams, Janet Thomae, Chris
  Maddock & one hundred and six graduates of Wizard Academy.
      p.   cm.
  ISBN 1-885167-54-7
  1. English language—Rhetoric. 2. Description (Rhetoric)
3. Photography—Literary collections. 4. Photography in education.
5. Visual perception. 6. Report writing. I. Williams, Roy H. II.
Thomae, Janet, 1975– III. Maddock, Chris, 1972–

PE1427 .A24 2001
808'.042—dc21   2001043698

The author may be contacted at the following address:

Roy H. Williams
Williams Marketing, Inc.
1760 FM 967
Buda, TX 78610
512-295-5700 voice, 512-295-5701 fax
www.WizardofAds.com

Credits
Managing Editor: **Janet Thomae**
Copy Editing: **Jeff Morris**
Proofreading: **Deborah Costenbader, Luke Torn**
Text Design/Production: **Hespenheide Design**
Jacket Design: **Hespenheide Design**
Cover Photograph: **Karen Titel (circa 1939)**

First printing: October 2001

Dedicated to the unnamed

Guatemalan boy in whose face

I saw such trust and hope

that bright July morning on the

streets of Antigua as I walked with

Eduardo Prado.

ROY H. WILLIAMS

To Richard Grosbard, for teaching us to see the magic in accidental snapshots.

To Kevin Randolph of krpix.com, for tirelessly digging through America's attics, closets, flea markets and estate sales in the hopes of finding more accidental magic.

To Karen Titel, who quietly gave us the miraculous cover shot of the two men walking through the revolving door. Karen, we know your name only because Kevin Randolph thought to ask, "Whose things were these that are being sold? What was the name of the woman who lived here?" Kevin wanted you to be remembered forever. And now you will be.

To Wizard Academy graduate Wendy McNally, who captured with her own talented finger the snapshots featured on pages 63 and 89.

To the 103 unnamed photographers whose fingers clicked 103 other shutters at precisely the right moment to capture these timeless images. How we wish we knew your names!

To all the graduates of the Academy who donated their time, energy, money and words to benefit the gentle people of Guatemala.

Dear Reader,

Have you ever been so captivated by a photo that you wondered what was happening the moment it was captured? Ever imagine what the subject was thinking or what was going through the mind of the photographer?

Once a month, people travel from around the world to attend Wizard Academy, the acclaimed school of innovative communication skills and creative thought located just outside Austin, Texas. Academy alumni include journalists, college professors, ministers, small business owners, corporate CEOs, and executives from many of the world's largest advertising firms.

Upon graduation, each student is challenged to create a literary snapshot inspired by the Wizard's collection of amateur photography. The Wizard tells us, "A photograph is a window through which we can peer into another world." Throughout the pages of this book, his students narrate a guided tour of these "other worlds."

For one year, my electronic in-box has overflowed with submissions from anxious graduates hoping to be featured in this book. My assignment: to nurture and encourage them in their writing. (Some students submitted to me 30 to 40 times before being selected. I'm hoping that these people are still talking to me!) 1,751 emails later, I've chosen the best 106 interpretations to share with you. Hopefully, you'll find this book to be instructional and entertaining, because if it sells as well as we hope it will, the royalties will allow us to do many more wonderful things for the very deserving people of Guatemala.

Accidental Magic is the first business book of its kind; one you can just sit back and enjoy.

Are you sitting back?

Fantastic!

Janet Thomae
Managing Editor

Your first impression of Eduardo Prado is that he would make the perfect Latin James Bond. Your second impression is that he beams enough positive energy to be a Spanish Rick Dees. But it was only after seeing Eduardo interact with Guatemala's poorest people that the third and final image of him peeked over the horizon of my mind.

This fleeting glimpse happened on the sidewalk outside the hotel where Eduardo and I had met only a few minutes earlier. After pausing to introduce me to a young Guatemalan boy, perhaps fourteen years old and obviously quite poor, Eduardo stared deeply into the young man's eyes, placed his fingers on the boy's cheek, and spoke to him very quietly and fervently in Spanish. When Eduardo was finished, the boy smiled softly and nodded with confidence. Eduardo then gently patted the boy's cheek and they parted. In that singularly tender and majestic moment, I was reminded, not so much of James Bond or Rick Dees as of England's fabled King Arthur.

"What did you say to him?" I asked. Eduardo said, "I told him that he was an extremely smart young man and that he had a very bright future and that he should never quit believing in it." After a moment of silence, Eduardo continued, "He is a student in a class that I teach." "What kind of class?" I asked. Eduardo looked at me thoughtfully and said, "Are you familiar with the saying, 'Give a man a fish and he eats for a day, teach him to fish and he eats for a lifetime?'" I nodded that I was. Eduardo then smiled a tearful smile and said, "I teach the poor how to escape their poverty."

When Eduardo Prado made me a knight, he was obviously hoping that the Guatemalan people would become very dear to me and that I would do my best to help him help them.

He was right. We are doing all that we can to help. But our motive isn't tied to any appreciation of the knighthood (although I do enjoy signing my name "Sir Roy" once in awhile.) We help Eduardo Prado because I once saw him lay his hand on the cheek of a poor Guatemalan boy and promise that boy a bright future.

We just want to make sure that Eduardo can keep that promise.

Your purchase of this book moves us one small step closer to that goal as 100 percent of all royalties are being donated toward that effort.

Thank you for helping.

I dearly wish you had seen that boy's smile.

Roy H. Williams

PART I

CONCEPTS

Chapters 1 – 8

These chapters are contributed by Roy H. Williams, theorist behind Wizard Academy. He is renowned for teaching innovative communication skills to CEOs of large companies, small business owners, and journalists around the world. Inspired by great artists from all disciplines, Roy describes how you can incorporate their genius into your writing.

CHAPTER 1

WHERE WILL YOU SHOW YOUR MENTAL MOVIE?

Your body contains nearly 100 million sensory receptors that enable you to see, hear, taste, touch, and smell physical reality. But your brain contains more than 10,000 billion synapses. In other words, you are about 100,000 times better equipped to experience a world that does not exist than a world that does. A person can do nothing that they have not first seen themselves do in their mind. The objective of human persuasion is to cause that person to imagine doing what you want them to do.

Fact and fiction both happen in your brain, which is divided into two main sections called hemispheres. Your right brain is intuitive and subjective. It sees the "big picture"; it's where you appreciate music and the arts. Your left brain is logical, linear, and objective; it focuses on details. It is the left brain that, through your senses, gathers and stores facts about the world around you.

Each hemisphere of your brain contains a mental movie screen. In your right brain, that screen provides an awesome, 360-degree global vista that extends above, below, and all around you. Watching this mental movie screen is like floating weightlessly in the middle of a vast, translucent bubble with a million glowing scenes bouncing off its inner walls. Warm, dazzling colors reach out to you from each image. Twisting and turning in every direction, you see amazing new things from each new perspective. Unfortunately, your right brain is nonverbal, so you must find the words to express all this within the tight confines of your brain's left half.

The sad little movie screen of your left brain is much too small to reveal anything grand. It shows only flat (two-dimensional), black-and-white images. As if that weren't bad enough, a legalistic little theater manager insists that every complex concept be broken down into its component parts so that they can be examined separately on the left brain's little black-and-white screen.

Doubt is what happens when the security guard of the rational, logical left brain isn't sure whether or not to accept an idea. The right brain, however, is not troubled by such issues. It isn't concerned in the least about the plausibility of an idea; that's a judgment it's happy to leave to the left brain. So when your idea is rejected at the door of the left brain, just knock on Righty's door; he'll let anyone in. Once inside the mind, your idea can scoot over to the logical left brain on the waterslide of symbolic thought.

According to Dr. Ricardo Gattass of the Institute of Biophysics, all human thought can be classified as verbal, abstract, analytical, or symbolic.

1. In verbal thought, we experience ideas as if listening to our own voice. Using auditory memory, we translate ideas into words. Verbal thought is a left-brain process.

2. In analytical thought, we examine possibilities in a logical sequence. The goal? To see the future. The objective of analytical thought is to predict results. Obviously, analytical thought is left brain.

3. Abstract thought is right brain and is utterly free. In abstract thought, intuition and emotion replace logic as we examine ideas and sensory experiences. The mental images created in abstract thought are unbounded by the physical world and often represent imaginary events.

4. In symbolic thought, we assess a thing from different perspectives. Musical understanding is symbolic thought, as are similes and metaphors. We use symbolic thought to encode and decode associative memories. Symbolic thought bridges intuition and intellect, right brain and left. Symbolic thought is the key that opens both heart and mind.

There is a way to speak to the right brain and a way to speak to the left, with each technique using symbolic thought. In the chapters to come, we'll show you exactly how to do these things.

The greatest teacher who ever lived used symbolic thought in 100 percent of his presentations. His use of simile and metaphor was legendary. He was forever saying things like "The kingdom of heaven [a right-brain, abstract concept] is like a mustard seed [a left-brain, factual concept]."

CHAPTER 2

SURPRISING BROCA

When Americans are bored or in a funk, we say we've "got the blues." An Israeli will say she is "meduchdach," while an Italian will be "scoraggiato." A Japanese person calls this feeling "yuutsu"; a German will say he is "niedergeschlagen." The American expression is the only one that refers to a color, yet each of these people is trying to describe exactly the same feeling. The mental image of boredom and mild depression is the same for each of them; they have simply attached different sounds to it. Neurologists tell us that such wordless mental images are the universal language of all humankind.

But if the whole human family thinks in the same language, then why do we speak in so many different ones?

According to cognitive neuroscience, human thought is a speed-of-light progression of mental images, each one a complex composite of sound, shape, texture, color, smell, taste, and mood. Languages are created when different sounds are attached to these mental images in Wernicke's area, a specialized part of the left brain.

Once a word has been attached to each mental image, the whole verbal jigsaw puzzle moves to Broca's area, where the selected words are arranged into understandable sentences. Only after the puzzle is assembled in Broca's area are we finally able to "speak our mind."

When Wernicke attaches the "usual" words and Broca arranges them in the "usual" order, the result can be painfully predictable: "Merlot is more full-bodied than Cabernet." But a little extra effort by Wernicke and Broca changes this boring sentence into an electric one: "Cabernet tastes of sunshine and rainbows, while Merlot is foggy, dark, and Gothic." Now everyone at the table is scrambling to have a taste.

While the speaker uses Broca to arrange his words into understandable sentences, the listener uses Broca to anticipate and discount the predictable. When your listener hears only what she expects to hear, it's virtually impossible to keep her attention.

When speaking or writing, think of Broca as the movie critic who will decide whether or not to walk out on your movie. To gain Broca's smiling approval and win the attention of the reader or listener, you must electrify Broca with the thrill of the unexpected. "More full-bodied" just won't do.

Such language causes Broca to be "niedergeschlagen."

CHAPTER 3

FROSTING

Named after the poet Robert Frost, "Frosting" is the simplest and gentlest technique for transforming drab communication into razor-edged wordsmanship.

The essence of Frosting is to replace common, predictable phrases with unexpected, interesting ones. The goal is simply to surprise Broca with elegant combinations of words.

To better understand Frosting, we'll de-Frost Robert Frost's powerful poem "Misgiving." Compare the language in the de-Frosted poem below with the corresponding phrases in the original, fully Frosted version that follows it.

> The leaves all shouted, "We will go with you, O wind!"
> They said they would follow him to the end.
> But they got sleepy as they went along,
> So they tried to convince him to stay with them.
>
> Ever since they got started way back last spring
> The leaves had been looking forward to this flight,
> But now they would rather hide behind a wall
> Or lie under some bushes to spend the night.
>
> And now when the wind yells at them to come along,
> They answer him with less and less vigor.
> At most they just move around a little,
> But they don't move very fast. Go figure.
>
> I'd like to believe that when I am dead,
> And can finally find out what there is to it,
> And learn all the mysteries beyond the grave
> That I won't be like them . . . too tired to do it.

De-Frosted, the story has the feel of those tacky little third-grade limericks, doesn't it?

Now let's read the poem as Frost originally wrote it. Take note of the vivid, concise mental images created through Frost's unusual combinations of common words, and how he plunges you quickly into the action with an early verb.

> All crying, "We will go with you, O Wind!"
> The foliage follow him, leaf and stem;
> But a sleep oppresses them as they go,
> And they end by bidding him stay with them.
>
> Since ever they flung abroad in spring
> The leaves had promised themselves this flight,
> Who now would fain seek sheltering wall,
> Or thicket, or hollow place for the night.
>
> And now they answer his summoning blast
> With an ever vaguer and vaguer stir,
> Or at utmost a little reluctant whirl
> That drops them no further than where they were.
>
> I only hope that when I am free
> As they are free to go in quest
> Of the knowledge beyond the bounds of life
> It may not seem better to me to rest.

Who, then, will teach us to persuade? Who can teach us to transfer an entirely new perspective in a brief, tight economy of words? Is there a writer whose stated goal is to cause us to see things differently?

Ah, the poet.

Poetry is not about rhyming. It is about unusual combinations of unpredictable words that surprise Broca and gain the voluntary attention of the listener. It is about transferring a new perspective.

The simplest way to improve your communication skills is to read a poem a day. Absorb them like daily vitamins and you will soon be free of the disease of verbal predictability.

Exercise: Find something of at least a few paragraphs that you've written, and, without changing the message structurally, replace all the common, predictable phrases with unexpected, interesting ones. Whip a little Frosting on it.

CHAPTER 4

SEUSSING

LIFE magazine, April 6, 1959: "If you should ask [Dr. Seuss] how he ever thought up an animal called a Bippo-no-Bungus from the wilds of Hippo-no-Hungus or a Tizzle-Topped Tufted Mazurka from the African island of Yerka, his answer would be disarmingly to the point: 'Why, I've been to most of those places myself, so the names are from memory. As for the animals, I have a special dictionary which gives most of them, and I just look up their spellings.'"

The technique I call "Seussing" is simply making up your own new words. Do you have the courage to do it? Nothing delights Broca quite so much as instinctively knowing the meaning of a word that he's never before heard. Sitting in the tollbooth of the brain, the ever-watchful Broca hates predictability, but he's always delighted by the elegant unexpected.

Dr. Seuss understood the danger of predictability. Though each of his stories had a moral, he was careful never to start with one. "Kids," he said, "can see a moral coming a mile off and they gag at it." Dr. Seuss allowed each story's moral to develop on its own. Never was it forced or contrived. When a writer is surprised by the ending of his own story, and by the moral message it contains, you can bet the reader will be, too.

Another function of Broca's area is to attach imagined actions to the words you and I call verbs. Since Broca guards the door leading into the imagination, it only stands to reason that verbs are more important to persuasion than nouns, words that are attached to persons, places, and things in Wernicke's area at the other end of the brain. Seuss somehow knew this intuitively. In *Pipers at the Gates of Dawn*, Jonathan Cott describes meeting a seventy-six-year-old Dr. Seuss in July 1980 and discussing with him the work of Kornei Chukovsky, a Russian children's poet who in 1925 wrote a book about how to win and hold their attention. One of Chukovsky's strongest suggestions in the book was to "avoid using too many adjectives and, instead, to use more verbs." Seuss emphatically agreed.

Likewise, the good doctor understood that to win the voluntary attention of young children (the world's most inattentive audience), he would need to enter the realm of the illogical, nonjudgmental right brain first, then proceed to the rational, logical left. Dr. Seuss books proceed from the simple premise that children will believe a ludicrous situation if it is pur-

See Seussing on pages 69, 143 and 186.

sued with relentless logic. "If I start with a two-headed animal," said Seuss, "I must never waver from that concept. There must be two hats in the closet, two toothbrushes in the bathroom, and two sets of spectacles on the night table. Then my readers will accept the poor fellow without hesitation and so will I."

Will you dive — splash! — into the right brain before swimming over to the left? Are you paying close attention to your verbs? Do you have the audacity to moon predictability by using a word that's not official? Seussing, like pepper sauce, is powerful. A tiny bit adds zip to even the blandest of dishes.

Seuss up your writing; use a word they've never heard.

> "Mrs. Sloan!" he called out at last. After another minute, the innkeeper leaned out through the kitchen door.
>
> "Oh, my, there you are," she exclaimed, wiping her hands on her apron. "I was just making tonight's soup."
>
> "I'm sorry to bother you, but I wanted to give you back the keys to your car. Thank you."
>
> "Think nothing of it." She took them and threw them into a **battered metal** cash box just below the liquor bottles. "Now, what can I get you to drink?" She **lumbered** behind the bar, filling the space **like a battleship in a canal.** [Frosting, Frosting, Frosting]
>
> "I'll have a . . . " Hal stopped, unable to **squeeze** [**Frosting**] the words out of his mouth. . . .
>
> "Oops, I hear the soup boiling over." She turned and fled, with a certain **rhinoceroid grace** [**Seussing**], into the kitchen.

— From chapter 38 of *The Forever King*, by Molly Cochran and Warren Murphy

CHAPTER 5

BEING MONET

Blurry, bright, Impressionist paintings aren't about details or accuracy. In fact, Claude Monet said that he hoped "to capture the first impression of an image; that moment before the eye or camera focused." He said he was striving for "instantaneity."

In 1869, Monet was painting at La Grenouillère when he realized that shadows are not just black or brown but are influenced by their surrounding colors. He further realized that the

> **color** of an object is modified by the
> > **light** in which it is seen, by
> > > **reflections** from other objects, and by
> > > > **contrast** with juxtaposed colors.

Likewise, the meaning of a word is influenced by the surrounding words. The

> **color** of a word is modified by the
> > **light** (context) in which it is seen, by
> > > **reflections** from words near it, and by
> > > > **contrast** with words juxtaposed to it.

Monet considered black to be the total lack of color: "Though shadows are darker than surrounding colors, they still contain some degree of color. Therefore, shadows are not black." As a result, Monet virtually eliminated void, empty black from his palette of paints.

When Monet minimized his use of black, his remaining colors sprang to life.

> **Light** radiated from his canvas.
> > **Reflections** became luminous.
> > > **Contrasts**, magical.
> > > > **Images**, worth million$.

Likewise, to speak Monet, you must eliminate empty, void "black words" from your sentences. Light will radiate from the words remaining. Persuasion will become luminous. Results, magical. Refine this, and you will own a talent worth million$.

Look for outstanding examples of Moneted writing on pages 40, 59 and 73.

The fundamental principles of being Monet:

1. Ignore the details.
2. Exaggerate the color.
3. Remove the black.

It's not about making perfect sense. It's right-brain language, impressionistic and dazzling.

> I was born and grew up in Baltic marshland
> by zinc-grey breakers that always marched on
> in twos. Hence all rhymes, hence that wan flat voice
> that ripples between them like hair still moist,
> if it ripples at all. Propped on a pallid elbow,
> the helix picks out of them no sea rumble
> but a clap of canvas, of shutters, of hands, a kettle
> on the burner, boiling — Lastly, the seagull's metal cry.

— Opening lines of "A Part of Speech"
Joseph Brodsky, Poet Laureate of the United States, 1992–1996

CHAPTER 6

POWER MONET

Perhaps the definitive writer of "Monet" in our generation is the great Paul Simon. To all who would follow him into the electric wonderland of literary Impressionism, he offers this advice:

> If you want to write a song about the moon, walk along the craters of the afternoon when the shadows are deep and the light is alien and gravity leaps like a knife off the pavement. If you want to write a song about the heart, think about the moon before you start, because the heart will howl like a dog in the moonlight and the heart can explode like a pistol on a June night. So if you want to write a song about the heart and its ever-longing for a counterpart, write a song about the moon.
>
> Hey, songwriter, if you want to write a song about a face, think about a photograph that you really can't remember . . . but can't erase. Wash your hands in dreams and lightning. Cut off your hair, and whatever is frightening, if you want to write a song about a face. If you want to write a song about the human race, write a song about the moon. If you want to write a song about the moon . . . if you want to write a spiritual tune . . . then do it. . . . Write a song about the moon.
>
> — Paul Simon's advice to writers in "Song about the Moon," from his album *Hearts and Bones* © 1981, Warner Bros. Records

You should go buy this CD if you don't already own it.

CHAPTER 7

FRAMELINE MAGNETISM

Muskogee, Oklahoma, 1965, Hilldale Elementary School, Mrs. Shelton's second-grade class: One by one, we march to the front of the room to recite the poems we've written. It's Reggie Gibson's turn. "Spider, Spider, on the wall. Ain't you got no smarts at all? Don't you know that wall's fresh plastered? Get off that wall, you dirty . . . (long pause) spider." The class explodes. Mrs. Shelton is not amused. Reggie Gibson has discovered frameline magnetism.

The edge of a picture is called the frameline. When an image extends beyond the frameline, the viewer's imagination reacts by filling in what was left outside the frame. This phenomenon is called frameline magnetism, and it's a powerful tool that has long been used by the world's great photographers, videographers, filmmakers, and illustrators to engage the imagination of a viewer.

The first time I ever used verbal frameline magnetism was in an ad for my first client, Woody Justice. I had written almost verbatim what Woody had said to me on the phone in a moment of frustration. Then, looking at what I was holding, I saw the core of a powerful radio script that would become a true pouring-out of Woody's heart to the public. I didn't want to shatter the intimate moment by jamming the store's address and phone number into the ad, so I persuaded Woody to let me leave them out. At the end of the ad, when listeners were expecting the predictable blah, blah, blah of a store address and phone number, they heard only a moment's pregnant pause, then Woody saying off-mike: "Okay, I'm done." And that was all.

Radio listeners were stunned by what wasn't there. Although it's been well over a decade, people in Missouri still talk about that ad.

That which is not spoken often speaks the loudest.

"Talk low, talk slow, and don't say too much."

— John Wayne's advice to actors

CHAPTER 8

BEING PERFECTLY (ROBERT) FRANK

Robert Frank is generally regarded as one of the greatest photographers the world has ever seen. In his legendary photo book, *The Americans*, Frank captures the unposed reality of 1955–56 America with such ruthless clarity that collectors now bid tens of thousands of dollars to own just one of his vintage prints.

At the drive-in theater, Robert Frank would be in the car behind you, aiming his camera through the windshield to capture what it felt like to be at a drive-in movie at sundown. At the political rally, Frank wasn't interested in the practiced smile of the up-and-coming politician, but would take his photos from behind the man in a way that made you feel the pressure that was on the candidate and sense the energy in the air. At the opera on opening night, when all the other photographers were crowded into "the one good spot to shoot from," Robert Frank would be down in the orchestra pit, letting you see what the conductor was seeing and making you feel what the conductor was feeling.

Robert Frank was (1) unusual in his selection of an angle, (2) economical in his inclusion of detail, and (3) a master of frameline magnetism. Isn't it interesting that these are precisely the same three techniques that Ernest Hemingway used to become one of the most respected novelists in history?

Speaking of the unusual angle, or perspective, from which he typically approached a story, Hemingway once said, "In stating as fully as I could how things really were, it was often very difficult and I wrote awkwardly and the awkwardness is what they called my style. All mistakes and awkwardness are easy to see, and they called it style."

In his photographs, Robert Frank excluded all but the barest and most necessary elements. Likewise, Hemingway's writing style was economical, using simple words to create detached, impersonal descriptions of action that captured the scene precisely. Simple details in black and white, no romantic exaggeration. Like Frank, Hemingway was deeply concerned with authenticity. His goal was to provide readers with the raw material of an actual experience.

Here's how Hemingway described frameline magnetism: "I always try to write on the principle of the iceberg. There is seven-eighths of it under

> "Poor Faulkner. Does he really think big emotions come from big words? He thinks I don't know the ten-dollar words. I know them all right. But there are older and simpler and better words, and those are the ones I use."
>
> — Ernest Hemingway

Look for outstanding examples of Franked writing on pages 58, 79 and 226.

water for every part that shows. Anything you know you can eliminate and it only strengthens your iceberg. It is the part that doesn't show."

Principles of Being Perfectly (Robert) Frank

1. Choose a revealing angle. Put the reader/listener/viewer on the scene.
2. Select your details sparingly. Include only what's interesting. And barely that.
3. Put the known "under water." Never tell the reader/listener/viewer anything he already knows or can figure out for himself.

To write Robert Frank is to communicate in the fewest words and from the most interesting perspective. It's how to speak to the left brain with accuracy and clarity without being boring.

WIZARD ACADEMY DEFINITIONS

Frosting: replacing common, predictable phrases with unexpected, interesting ones.

being Monet: speaking impressionistically, rather than precisely, by using poetic exaggeration and overstatement and selecting words according to the intensity of their associations, or "color." To speak in incomplete sentences due to the removal of "black words." Being Monet might be thought of as radical, accelerated Frosting.

instantaneity: engaging the imagination with a vivid and electric first mental image (FMI).

black words: words that do not contribute toward a more vivid and colorful mental image (but, and, that, therefore, etc.)

Daguerre: a derogatory term, used to describe a style of writing that is factual, tedious, and colorless. Most academic writing is "Daguerre."

Robert Frank: a style of writing that is accurate, but very selective in its inclusion of detail, and that approaches the subject from an unusual angle.

putting it under water: editing or deleting information under the assumption that it is already known to the listener.

PART II

APPLICATIONS

Chapters 9 – 16

These chapters are contributed by Chris Maddock, the Wizard's first assistant. Professor Maddock explains how to say more, and say it better, in fewer words. His notes are taken from lessons taught at Wizard Academy. They are the instructional pieces used by the students to create the magical literary snapshots you will experience in part III.

CHAPTER 9

WRITING TO THE INTUITIVE

I enter REM sleep at the exact velocity necessary for the movie camera in my head to project coherent images. My brain is replaying scenes from the 1990 Cannes Film Festival Winner, *Wild at Heart,* directed by weirdo-genius David Lynch. The images are fuzzy, and my brain fast-forwards past Cage and Dern's middling acting, past the scenes oversaturated with color, past the stiff violence. Milliseconds before I awake, the real meat of my mental stew becomes clear. With hyperdigital clarity my brain focuses on an image: full frame, a flame ignites the anxious end of a cigarette in a crackling hiss that sounds like a bonfire. If you've seen the movie, you remember. Lynch uses the cigarette lighting over and over, like a page break, or the Superfriends' logo when the announcer says, "Meanwhile, back at the Hall of Justice. . . ."

Lynch's cigarette lighting is just a little thing that doesn't fit, and it takes one completely off guard. Yet at some insane, subpsychological level, it does fit. The creative, intuitive right side of the brain kicks in and says, "Yeah, man!" at the same time the strictly intellectual left brain is asking Lynch to clarify things.

I saw *Wild at Heart* once, over ten years ago, on a date with a girl I hardly knew, and I remember the constant cigarette lighting perfectly. My brain understands. Roger Ebert's does, too. But he doesn't know why: "I don't think it is a very good film. There is something repulsive and manipulative about it, and it has the flavor of a kid in the schoolyard trying to show you pictures you don't feel like looking at. I was angry, as if a clever con man had tried to put one over on me."

I betcha Roger always looked at those pictures. And remembered them. Because before Roger was paid and applauded for being a mainly left-brained critic, he was a mainly right-brained kid.

CHAPTER 10

KEEP'EM CURIOUS

(sfx: sound of machines. Gets louder)

(guy's voice)

All right, Jack, let's have a look-see. . . . C'mon. . . . There ya go. Okay, you're spinnin' now, baby. Oh, you're blindin' me, uh huh.

(slowly)

Yeah, now get ready for the big gear shifter. . . . Focus on the lineup.

Show me the big J. Flash me across the road, Jackie P.

(excited)

I'm feelin' you, babe!

(machine starts to slow)

Oh, well, excuse me. Hey, it's you, Cherry. I didn't know you were interested in playin'. Hmm. Okay, then. Make me a free man. You're lookin' good, girl. How about a peekaboo from YOU! That's it. . . . You make apples jealous. Now, put the brakes on it, hon. There you go. Big daddy's gonna be makin' some pie tonight! Cherry! Cherry! Cherry! Cherry!

(machine comes to a stop)

YES! Haaaaa! I won. . . . Hey, hand me another bucket. Hello? Me. Winner here. Ha ha!!

(sfx: ding ding ding: change flows)

ANNCR: The hottest slots anywhere. Clearwater Casino . . . where the REAL casino action flows.

In almost every Academy, I ask, "What was the last movie you paid to see twice?" It was probably a movie like this ad. One that made you curious. One that was interesting even though you didn't know exactly what was happening until the end of the movie. In fact, in an ad like this, written by March 2001 graduate Kelly Bridges-Studer, not knowing makes the initial monologue all the more interesting. Broca's area of the brain is called to full attention because everything that's happening is unexpected, novel, and therefore intriguing. The next time you heard this ad, you'd turn up the radio. Wouldn't you like people to turn up your ads?

CHAPTER 11

WHAT BROCA WANTS

Our last Academy Notes gave you an intriguing, compelling example of Moneted writing. This prompted several of you to ask for an equally commendable Franked piece. I found dozens that warranted mention, but this one, written by November 2000 graduate Shelby Reddick Branzanti, is particularly interesting:

> I love big houses, high ceilings, big bay windows, leaded glass. You know . . . the kind that cry, "I have money." Many would say that one who thinks this way is pretentious . . . puts himself above everyone else. Okay. That's me. I *am* better than everyone else. When I put my mind to having a house like this, I always get my way. I visualize the French doors, the openness and space that money creates, and I know exactly how to get inside. It's easy. A quick cut, a flick, and I'm in. Yup, I love the kind of house that yells, "I have money!"
>
> Chubb Security Systems. 1-800-88CHUBB. When you're not home, they are.

Exactly like the Moneted ad, much of what makes this Franked ad so interesting would also make most clients and ad writers nervous: you don't immediately know what the ad is about; the company is mentioned only once, and at the end to boot; and there's no "close" or call to action. The ad doesn't sound like an ad. In fact, there's a chance the first time a listener hears this ad he won't know exactly what's happening. But you're not nervous. You know that the next time this ad comes over the radio or TV, the listener or viewer will turn up the volume. You understand that if you have a solid, long-term presence, ads like these will not be completely digestible the first time. You know that this is a good thing.

CHAPTER 12

AN IRRESISTIBLE MYSTERY

In *The Crossing*, National Book Award winner Cormac McCarthy brings his young protagonist to the hut of an old Mexican man to find out how to capture a wolf:

> The boy said that the wolf of which he spoke was in fact herself a shewolf and he asked if that fact should figure in his strategies against her but the old man only said that there were no more wolves.
>
> Ella vino de Mexico, the boy said.
>
> He seemed not to hear. He said that Echols had caught all the wolves.
>
> El señor Sanders me dice que el señor Echols es medio lobo es mismo. Me dice que él conoce lo que sabe el lobo antes de que lo sepa el lobo. But the old man said that no man knew what the wolf knew.
>
> His breath had gone wheezy from his exertions. He coughed quietly and lay still. After a while he spoke again.
>
> Es cazador, el lobo, he said. Cazador. Me entiendes?
>
> The boy didn't know if he understood or not. The old man went on to say that the hunter was a different thing than men supposed. He said that men believe the blood of the slain to be of no consequence but that the wolf knows better. He said that the wolf is a being of great order and that it knows what men do not: that there is no order in the world save that which death has put there.

We've spoken about making things irresistible by adding a bit of mystery. Mr. McCarthy understands this instinctively. He knows that more than 90 percent of his English-speaking audience will not literally or completely understand the Spanish passages above. Yet to leave them in Spanish puts us in the mind of the boy, who also does not know whether he understands or not. It is obvious that this obliqueness is intended; McCarthy takes pains to explain certain things in English, yet clouds others with his Spanish. It is little wonder I'm reading the book for a second time.

Is this a tactic that would work in your radio, television, or print ads? Quizas usted debe darle un intento!

CHAPTER 13

SHOWING AND TELLING

Good writing should show, not tell. This is true whether the appeal is made to the intellect or the emotion. Intellectual ads that tell by making unsubstantiated claims lack believability:

> The new Italo Monza 5 is the fastest, most agile European sports car ever.

So you say, the listener thinks, unmoved.

> The new Italo Monza 5 rockets to 60 miles per hour in 4.3 seconds, faster than a Porsche 911, and its lateral acceleration can produce an overwhelming 1.3 g's.

Geez, that's a fast, agile car, the listener realizes.

Likewise, ineffective emotional ads fail to create a credible reality when they tell instead of show. This is especially true of poorly written, second-person, "experiential" ads:

> You put your fingers on the grip of your new Big Eagle Driver. You're confident in its solid, balanced feel. Eyeing the windblown fairway, you're nervous, but excited. You swing. As the ball plops down dead center, you feel like the happiest golfer on earth.

Yeah, you've brought me to the golf course, but that wasn't me. . . . I wasn't feeling those things.

> You grasp your new Big Eagle Driver. Your fingers fall softly, naturally into grip. Your first practice swing fluid and effortless. Your heart slows, then your breathing. Somehow, the windblown fairway seems bigger today. You take a last, long breath. You swing. As the ball plops down dead center, you look at your partner and say, "Hey, Buddy, how you feel about playin' 36 today?"

Mmmm, sounds like the Big Eagle Driver will give me confidence, and in the end make me a happier golfer.

To show is to be patient. To show is to have faith in your ability and faith in your audience. Do you have faith yet?

CHAPTER 14

THE RHYTHM OF YOUR WRITING

What's the rhythm of your writing? If you can say what it is, that's a good thing. If you can't because you're aware that it varies, that's even better.

The ads you compose contain a finite number of words. As we've discussed, there are several tools you can use to extend meaning, aura, and feeling with the same number of words. Words with robust associations do just this. So does the rhythm of your writing. The most powerful writing matches its rhythm to the feeling and scene it intends to create. If you aim to inspire an excited, fast-moving feeling in your listener, do so with the rhythm of your writing:

> Suddenly you're racing through a tunnel of trees blurring past in streaks of varying green on a rail of smooth rubber. Knees and feet and arms and body melded to the purring cycle pouring its happiness into you and the countryside about.

Notice how kinetic verbs, lean nouns, and scant punctuation breathe energy into this passage — all without the help of a shouting voiceover.

With a different rhythm, you can make your listener feel relaxed and sleepy: "Beyond the porch and up the draw a bit, you see the aspens quake like thousands of reverent pews in the near distance. Green, gold, green. Your neighbor-birds converse only in hushed murmurment . . . often, it seems, choosing a lull of wind and its matching calm to share their thoughts." Abundant punctuation and descriptives, along with close attention to detail, help slow the rhythm and lend a sense of restfulness.

Be aware of the rhythm of your writing. Test yourself. Pick a mood and try to match it with your diction. Do so, and your ads will become magical.

CHAPTER 15

HOW TO COLOR YOUR WRITING

You've tried to help your listener fully realize the actions and emotions in your ad writing: more showing, less telling. Yet sometimes you fail to impart enough of an experience. You find yourself wanting to tell the listener exactly how to feel.

Relax. Robert Frost can help.

> The shattered water made a misty din.
> Great waves looked over others coming in,
> And thought of doing something to the shore
> That water never did to land before.
> The clouds were low and hairy in the skies,
> Like locks blown forward in the gleam of eyes.
>
> — from "Once by the Pacific," by Robert Frost

Frost resists the impulse to tell the reader that this is a rather ominous scene. But by coloring his poem with nouns and descriptives that carry scary, portentous associations, he enables the reader to visualize and more deeply experience the scene.

To do the same, first choose an emotion or feeling to communicate, such as nervous excitement. Then think of some words or phrases you associate with that feeling: anxious, waiting, white-knuckled, hesitant, cold sweat. Now incorporate these into your writing:

> You step into your waiting car, failing to ward off the thought: "My first house." The seatbelt clutching your shoulder: "My first house." Engine hesitant, tires chirping, you drive white-knuckled through a cold sweat of rain toward a place you've been waiting to come home to your entire life.

Voilà! Color your ads with emotions. Enliven them with words fat with association. Don't just paint pictures — give rides.

CHAPTER 16

WRITE WHAT YOU KNOW

The ad writer is a blindfolded oddsmaker who begs attention from a man with no ears. Listen to his question: "Of what will I write?" He hears a remembered whisper: Write about what you know. "I know about my client's business," he says. But pen to paper produces ads about the business and not about the customer. "So what do I really know about the customer?" The same thing a poet or painter or novelist knows about his audience: their humanity, failings, and lots of little everyday things that make them smile. "But what does that have to do with the product or service?" Exactly.

> Good writing is true writing. If a man is making a story up
> it will be true in proportion to the amount of knowledge
> of life that he has and how conscientious he is; so that
> when he makes something up it is as it would truly be.
>
> — Ernest Hemingway

Poignant truth punches the listener in the stomach because mental BS is more repugnant than the real thing. Unpolluted truth is like smelling salts to Broca's area of the brain: the careful but silent negotiations for personal space on an elevator; the change you hear in your friend's voice when he finishes talking to his boss and turns to his beloved.

Cheers, "The Road Not Taken", *Full Metal Jacket,* and *The Adventures of Huckleberry Finn* aren't about bars, decisions made in the woods, war, or the Mississippi River. You can find their magic happening right outside your door.

"Doesn't finding a nugget of truth require a comedian's vigilance, a movie director's eye for truth? Doesn't it require risking something?"

You answer.

PART III

INTERPRETATIONS

What is *Accidental Magic*?

Inspired by the techniques taught at Wizard
Academy, the students have created literary
snapshots from Academy's amateur photography
collection. The students, business professionals
from some of the world's most successful corpo-
rations, are mastering techniques required to
imprint vivid mental imagery.

So, the magic in the photographs is accidental but the magic in the words . . . intentional.
Which snapshot do you suppose will be more
interesting?

Every spring, before planting their seeds, the bachelors gather at the east end of the park. Deliberately they maneuver through the crowd of townspeople, to where the eligible women wait with homemade wine.

To **sip** a woman's wine is to indicate interest. To swallow the entire cup is a proposal of marriage.

Lanky Vern Saunders has strolled the "goblet gauntlet" more times than any man. This afternoon, Annabelle Sweeny takes matters into her own hands. When Vern raises her sweet wine to his lips for the ninth year in a row, Annabelle holds her cup to his mouth until he finishes every drop.

ROB SELIGMANN

INTO HER OWN HANDS

SAY YOUR PRAYERS

My mom
my dad
my brothers
my sisters
my grandma and grandpa
all my uncles and aunts
my cousins, my friends
my teachers
my dog
my cat
my buddy monkey
and the food in the fallout shelter.

Amen

ROGER CURRIER

TRES Y CINCO

Cuando se seque el Hudson
tocaré la puerta de tu brownstone.
Quiero que me lleves a Greenwich Village
a tomar un café donde tú sabes.
Quiero que caminemos a lo largo de Bleecker
y que me cuentes cuentos de viejos gángsters.
En la esquina de la tercera y la cincuenta
quiero a las tres y cinco de la tarde
detener la ola humana y besarte.
Quiero almorzar contigo en el Stanhope
y desde allí ver a la gente
entrando y saliendo del museo.
Tomar un autobús hacia el downtown,
brunch en la octava avenida,
misa de doce en St. Peter's,
y Dios mirando para el otro lado . . .
(O. Henry no supo de nosotros,
y aunque hubiera sabido,
el sólo escribió historias que tuvieron finales.
La nuestra es como el East River.)

FIVE PAST THREE

When the Hudson dries up
I'll knock at the door of your brownston
I want you to take me to Greenwich Vill
to have a cup of coffee where you know.
I want us to walk the whole length of Bl
and I want you to tell me tales of old ga
At the corner of Third and Fiftieth
I want at five past three in the aftern
to stop the human wave and kiss you.
I want to have lunch with you at the Sta
and from there watch the people
going in and out of the museum.
Take a bus downtown,
brunch on Eighth Avenue,
noon mass at St. Peter's
and God looking the other way.
(O. Henry never knew anything about u
and even if he knew,
he only wrote stories that had endings.
Ours is like the East River.)

JUAN MANUEL G.

Of course she'll be back. What are you thinking?
They just take a long time when they go there.

It's going well. I think it's going well. It feels like it's
going well.

She laughed at the one about Kentucky. But I'm not
sure the laughter reached her eyes.

I don't know. But it feels like it's going good.
I think it's going good. It's going good, isn't it?

JIM RUBART

GOODBYE

It was the very next day that the fever began. Cheeks ablaze. Glassy stare. And I waited by his bed. His lips cried for a bit of water. His belly too sick to hold even a drop. He whimpered in the fog. I prayed for the sunshine to return to his eyes. I stayed by his bed and waited and prayed for him to get up and reach out a touch. I waited for the day we would race in the wet green grass and roll in sweet-smelling clover. I prayed. We had those days. We ran after balls. We greeted brand-new neighbors with a wag and a shake. And we prayed to the sunshine that blazed down from heaven for another day filled with our devotion. We lazed by fires, cuddled on the carpet and explored the streets and the streams in sun, snow and sleet. And we played and we prayed that each day would bring another.

Today I am sick and he sits by my bed. The warmth from my belly fails to reach my paws and he holds me and prays that my day will be easy. Someday we will look again into each other's eyes and run, tumbling down the hills and over the clouds and giggle and snuff and dance in the light.

KIRA AND EMILY LAFOND
Mother and Daughter

DOUBLE ROLANDO

My people were yapping about me. Monkey Boy chattered, "He's changed his routine." Desert Sands countered, "He's obsessed." Uma the Bubble Girl trilled, "He never smiles that much on the ground." My mole, George the Psycho, said I had become a topic. Indeed, since pulling into town my regime had been fatefully altered. I had my secret and it didn't take long for the weirds to butt heads and swell their ears. Talk, talk, talk, ricocheting glances, thoughts deflecting, contorting.

From where I perched every day, muscles stretched, it was hard not to smile. She returned daily at precisely five-fifteen. This wondrous creature gliding, twirling through her apartment, gracing an invisible partner. Stealing a glimpse every five and a half seconds, I saw her as a disjointed picture-card movie revealed by trembling hands. At the pendulum top, balancing the horizon, this angel was my true focus. Rewarding my patience, she butterflied towards her evening bath. Content once again, I performed my patented Double Rolando into the net as the gawking weirds disbanded.

JOHN A. WRIGHT

LOST

Our destination quietly beckoned as we were awakened by unknown feelings. The promise of a curious future drove our father's commitment to our travels. Despite fatigued eyes, we draped Old Fateful in our worth. Better days had passed as she sagged with despair. Jane, bound by her cart, stalled the adventure. As Dad hoisted her, he told of the past and the future we would not endure. Though short, his tale bore a glimpse of hope in Mom's eye. Spirits lifted, we closed fate's last door.

Too bad he didn't buy that map.

IAN LEIGHTON

Mercedes Beaudene had a tongue that could sting worse than a wet towel snapped, and T.C. loved her for it. Even back then he could wind her up tight as a top and send her spinning across the room as easy as saying good mornin'. None of us know what exactly it was that T.C. said or did to finally temper the storm that brewed within Mercedes. Oh don't misunderstand me now, the hurricanes still blow and tempers like lightning still flash across the face of the one and only Mercedes Beaudene. But once that passes, T.C. and Mercedes are like a soft summer breeze after an electrical storm gently pulling organza curtains back and forth like they're waltzing.

JACQUI MISENER

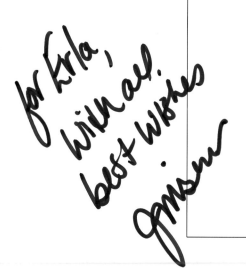

Aeons ago, before our dimensional flight,

Swirling round your smiling essence

Leaping from light,

With that familiar dive into time and space,

I reminded you I would find your face.

As promised, we see each other's eyes,

Past new disguises we have taken.

No need to comprehend some cosmic plan:

Only that when we awaken in brand-new lives,

Love survives.

Thinking they glimpsed a guileless kiss,

Thick grown-ups gush over our reunion's bliss.

A camera capturing what a child cannot explain:

How remembrance reappears . . .

How souls find each other again.

MONICA BALLARD

This is your **favorite** kitchen.
Your favorite kitchen in the whole wide world.

This is the kitchen that laughs.
Great big bellies full of laughter.
The kind of laughter that hurts your tummy and
makes your face ache.
That wonderful, painful, "please-make-it-stop"
laughter.

The most prized seats, of course, are around the
table. Or next to the wood stove.
But it doesn't matter where you sit, really. You can
hear the kitchen laughing all through the house.
Upstairs and down. Inside and out.
Frank said one night he could hear the kitchen
laughing all the way clear down to the Legion.

The funniest thing, though, is that it is pretty
much the same kitchen stories that get told
year after year.
Only, each time a story gets told, the kitchen
laughs even harder than the year before.
Then someone says, "Now, tell the one about . . ."
And Grandma interrupts, right on cue, saying,
"Oh, no! Not in front of Sister Ann!"

But the story gets told anyway. Again.
And the kitchen laughs. Again.
And you laugh. Again.
And Grandma laughs too.

Grandma is the best kitchen-laugher of all.
Nobody can out-laugh her. Not Uncle Leo.
Not Thea.
Not even Cousins Clifford, Victor, and Wilbert
combined.
Nobody laughs like your Grandma.

She is all of four-foot-nothin'.
But when she laughs, even the dishes shake.
And the world changes.
Forever.

This is your favorite kitchen.
Your favorite kitchen in the whole wide world.

SCOTT BRODERICK

HORMAN'S
HOME

Dear Mom,

1926 is a wonderful year!! This chrome and white beauty arrived today! I haven't used it yet, it's too lovely. Willie laughs, but I can't help it. It's our new baby, although not as cuddly as our real son, haha.

Today I finally used Horman. Gas is scary, I have to be careful not to get my apron over the flames. Tonight, baking bread, I'll sit in Grandpa's rocker and feel the glow from Horman's insides.

It's a sad night, Mom. Too much yeast made the bread throw up inside Horman's stomach. Cleaning removed some of the shine, and there are scratches in his bottom.

Today Willie tried to bake cookies. He left them in too long and they started on fire. The smoke ruined the front of Horman so he scrubbed it, hoping I wouldn't find out!! Imagine a man baking!! I don't know who I hate to look at more, Willie or scratched up Horman.

The mailman's here now.

Love from your daughter and soon-to-be-very-thin-because-his-wife-doesn't-cook-for-him-anymore son-in-law. Baby Jack, too.

SHELBY REDDICK BRANZANTI

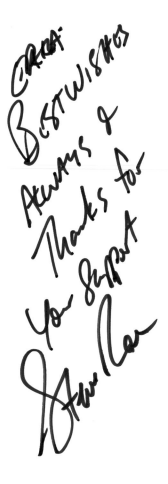

Fourteen years, every evening,
we ride the ferry like quivered
arrows. Skeltered nerves cooling
as we glide across the sound.
Comfort in comatonic routine,
same spot daily, same people.

You came one breath-hot day, tall
stovepipe frame loping over
deck. Your once proud suit now
hung like sad sack burlap. A face
jumbled like an impressionist's
palette; a capitol forehead above
cobalt eyes, nose aristocratically
topping a wide hayseed slash of
mouth. You sat down shaded
with statued stillness, no toes
rapping, nor hands squiggling,
long pencilled fingers quiet. Just
still. A quenching well of calm.

When I crossed your vision you
smiled. Time slowed,
evening surrendered. There
I was, washed clean with tran-
quility. Your smile endows a gift.

I watched for you again, but you
never came. So now I sit, just
still, endowing smiles too.

STEVE RAE

LUBED

In that final moment, **panic** overtook Phil like a bear chasing down its prey, as he realized that Bob had used too much hand lotion just before posing for this picture.

RICH MANN

SAVANNAH

Morning breaks over savannah green.

Delicate manilas **piccolo** in the breeze.

The scent of golden mist awakes the tawny meadow.

Treeless grasslands sway in amber waves.

A distant drumbeat. The chaotic staccato of Gazelle.

Bolt, leap, dart — a flight on Serengeti sands.

Hearts quicken . . . anticipating the lion.

Roar the earth, its Aztec bark.

Ivory tusks . . . hooves, kicking. Dark mustard clouds of tasteless dust.

Frenzied, bombastic flashes across the sky.

The glow of night falls. The turmeric delights.

MANDY BARCLAY

And then, one day I just gave up — well, not really in one day. It was really that summer (what a relief). I had tried to figure out what jokes to tell, when to tell them, and who to tell them to. My mom had finally bought me that Izod shirt, even though I really thought the lizard was kind of dumb. Oh yeah, it wasn't a lizard. It was an alligator — whatever. Then there was that time I brought my sister's Simon and Garfunkel album to school to play for one of the new kids, and the rest of the kids laughed at me. One of the girls said that I would be cool if I listened to Duran Duran. I wanted to like those bands, but I just couldn't.

It was so strange but wonderful that year and just a completely new feeling when I realized that, man, I guess I'm just different from everyone else, and that's okay.

DAVID NEVLAND

THE CHICKENS

CAMILA

Fast **asleep,** suddenly, dawn.

A loud noise awakens you; where are you?

What time is it? What's that sound?

Slowly it comes clearer. The phone, ringing.

What happened? What could it be?

Abruptly, bitterly, everything comes back.

Yes, it's her, your love, your life, your little miracle.

Frail, defenseless, precious, she who early arrived

Courageously fighting between life and death.

Have to rush to the hospital; your immediate presence is required.

Body performing its usual routine in no time — mind, somewhere else.

"Father, not my will, but Thine, be done."

Arrival, darkness, silence, sleepless people, slowness

An eternity until someone answers, protocol, bureaucracy.

"Our Father, Who art in Heaven, hallowed be Thy name . . ."
"Hail Mary full of Grace, the Lord is with thee."

Even the impossible is done, even the unacceptable is done.
Nothing, nothing is accomplished. Now she is with God.

Emptiness, tremendous emptiness.

Pain, indescribable pain.

Loneliness, gigantic loneliness.

Until now, you had no idea how deep you could fall into this abyss of sorrow.

Don't know what to do, what to say, what to feel, how to react.

"The Lord gave and the Lord has taken away; may the name of the Lord be praised."

"Goodbye my little love, goodbye my life. See you soon, if it is God's will."

JUAN GUILLERMO TORNOE

The rocks crackled as he raced near.

His rickety red truck sang the bad taste of a final tune.

The old green screen door creaked open and crashed three times shut.

The earth trembled from the thunder of his beat.

I felt the bumps swell beneath my skin.

Crackling knuckle sounds approached as a bottle ripped open.

My eyes grew teary with anticipation.

He flung the door open with reckless abandon.

I was helpless as he drew near.

There was nothing I could do.

My life will never be the same.

ANDY WINNIE

TAKE ME OUT . . .

It is much bigger than our 13-inch black-and-white set. The steamy blacktop parking lot oozes after the stampede of 11-year-old Cub Scouts races to see their heroes in person for the first time.

"Bring your glove," they said. "You might snag a homer." Harmon Killebrew has nothin' on us.

Left-field grandstand, upper deck, section 7, row 52, seat 14. The Minnesota Twins playing for me! A vibrant green checkerboard outfield. Achingly white balls hit across a silk-smooth chocolate-milk brown of the infield never take the crazy backyard hop like when my Dad hits them.

"Frosty Malt. How 'bout a Frosty Malt?" "Ice-cold beer here, bottle of beer." "Hot dogs, get your hot dogs." A cacophony of carnival barkers plying a banquet of goodies designed to spoil dinners and upset mothers.

The announcer booms out of the giant speakers, his voice reverberating through the stadium so you can feel it in your chest. "Now batting . . . Nummmmberrrrrrthreeeee . . . Harrrrrrmmonn Killlebrewwwwww."

Could he, will he, put one in the upper deck? You turn around. There it is! Two rows back. Painted red, white and blue. The seat Harmon Killebrew hit for his longest home run earlier that season.

Pay attention now. You tap your mitt twice for good luck and scream, "Come on Harmon!" He hears you. There's the set, the wind up, the pitch, he swings … Holy Cow!

TOM MOGUSH

67

TOY BOATS
AND SALTY
TEARS

When you're eight years old, you don't name your boat after a woman. Connor's was named after his boyhood companion, Libbie, our sad-eyed basset hound. He even painted her name on the small wooden hull. He loved that damn boat. Now whenever I see a boat, any boat, I see Connor. Like a Pavlovian dirty trick, my memoric projector starts running the same old 8mm black-and-white movie in my head. There's my little boy, sitting on our dock on the small lake behind our old house. Just like he'd done for years, hour upon hour, day after day, on his skinny knees watching his tiny toy boat glide through the water. The bright white mainsail and jib would fill with lake breezes as he'd daydream about sailing the seven seas. Eighteen years later, all they would find was a washed-up life-preserver, stenciled with the name "Libbie." Why couldn't I have given him the Stan Musial autographed glove for his birthday that year?

EMERSON "SKIP" ROBBINS

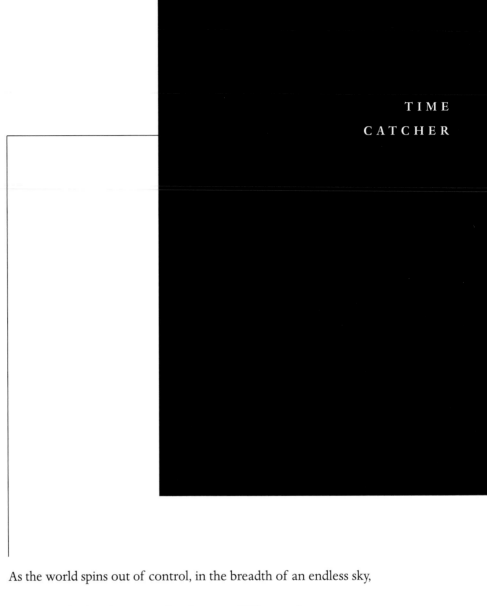

As the world spins out of control, in the breadth of an endless sky,

a moment in time is captured and a way of life gone by.

Tales of woe and wonder and portraits of a people unfold,

as storytellers pour their souls through young minds, undaunted and bold.

As buildings go up and buildings crumble,

the words once spoken, now so humble,

shall drum a silent vigil, until waters run dry

and time as we know it whispers good-bye.

KAREN COLETTA

The smell of **sugar** spun into clouds of pink, soles pulverizing peanut shells, wandering magically through the memories of childhood. A cacophony of snorts, whistles, screams, and squeals of delight echo and melt into a symphony of life. Rotting canvas barks in the howling wind, home to a menagerie of personalities and wildlife. Heavy machinery grinds the beat of progress, while bloated ropes pull spires of imagination into the sky. Dazzling swirls of rainbow colors brushed across sequins and feathers hide the reality from the fantasy, projecting deliciously different images in every mind's eye.

Joe Wallenda knew this was home . . . he could fly again.

STEVE COFFIN

73

December 24

Dear Diary,

Got home from the Christmas Eve service at church and you won't believe it. I opened the door — then twinkling chrome — flash-bulb shock — goose bumps — pine scent — Joy to the World! A heart-jolt hit — ker-THUMP! ker-THUMP! ker-THUMP! It nearly jumped right out of my body! I couldn't speak, breathe or even move for like eons. No telling what stupid look I had on my face. But who cares??!

There it was — all shiny and blue — white seat, white handlebar covers. The last thing I expected — the first thing on my secret list — the only thing I remember about tonight. It's the deepest, richest, brightest blue I've ever seen. And then, out of the corner of my eye, across the front fender, I saw Dad, beaming like a fool — flashing the Hawkeye camera — winding — changing the bulb — flashing again.

I'm still up — it's past midnight. I keep going back out there to be sure — I don't know if I'll ever get to sleep . . . my eyelids flip up like a jack-in-the-box every time I try. I never dreamed I'd get to have my very own bike. Wow! Wow! Wow!

Ya know, Diary, all that weird stuff Mom's been doing since school started? I mean like packing Daddy's and my lunches, letting down my hems, ironing Daddy's shirts. She even wore last year's dress to Daddy's office party, and taught three extra piano students — she's really been busy. And Daddy even fixed whatever-it-was that broke down on the car . . . and went out to Granny's ranch to chop down a fresh tree this year! Well now it all makes sense! They weren't scared we couldn't pay the bills, like I thought! They were getting ready for this . . . this . . . this amazing . . . supercalifragilisticexpialidocious . . . oh I just can't find the right words.

Wait'll I ride over to Peggy's tomorrow — I'm so **excited** — no more riding her brother's bike — Uck!

I don't think I'll ever forget those blinding flash bulbs! I'm going to make my bed every day, hang up my clothes, clean my room every Saturday, get all my homework done and never complain about washing up the dishes ever ever again!

ANDREA WELLS MILLER

Bessie was a nice gal. Always smiled at everybody. Didn't have no enemies. Perty too. Odd thing about her husband. Never did find out what happened for sure. But yeah, she was a nice gal. Took good care of her kids. Didn't even date for a long time. Just in case he came back. Shoulda stuck with that. That feller she did finally see a while, he was trouble. Jealous. She told him to leave her be. Guess he didn't wanna listen to her. She come home that night with a friend and pulled the cord to turn on the light. That's when she saw him. Even then, she was more worried about her friend. Told him to run. It was over perty quick. He run outta there and they found him sitting on the tracks a few miles away. Sure was a shame. Yep, that Bessie was a nice gal.

RENEE RICHARDSON

FOR A MOMENT

Every Friday I did my darndest to get their attention, I really did. But each would only watch for a moment, sometimes just a second. Sometimes the material wasn't interesting, sometimes the light pouring in from the overhead windows drowned my feeble attempts to capture their interest. Then there were the days when we had those really great pictures of the sunsets that Mr. Johnson brought, and some days we had a real heavy overcast and I really made them notice for a while, mostly just for a moment, but it was a glorious moment in the life of a slide projector in the 3rd grade.

PHIL STEWART

"What a wondrous age where those of us with class and means may travel the world simply to find the sun." Mother puts her book aside and waits for her daughter's reply.

"It's spring, dear. Don't you want to spend at least part of it in the States?"

"Nineteen-twelve can come and go for all I care. I'd be forever happy in the sun, the sand, and the south of France. What are you reading?"

"*Futility*, by Morgan Robertson."

"Is it good?"

"No, I'm afraid the news reads better than this man's fiction."

"Speaking of, did you hear there's talk of war in the Balkans?"

"Yes, but nothing will come of it. Your father says there'll be no more war."

"And why is that exactly?"

"Something to do with the resolve of the fighting man."

"Really?"

"That's what he says. Apparently the armies will no longer take the field in formation to meet the bullets rank and file."

"Are there none left willing to do their bit?"

"I don't believe it's courage. Rather, the repeating firearms of today would cause casualties to be horrendous, and the fighting man will no longer stand for it."

"No more wars."

"Precisely."

"It truly is a **wondrous** age we live in."

"Wondrous day anyway. It'll be a lot colder up north when we board. Oh I do hope your father remembered the tickets. THE TICKETS DEAR, DID YOU GET THE TICKETS?"

"THEY'RE IN THE BAG UNDER THE TOWELS!"

"I swear I remind that man of everything. He'd forget his — oh, here they are, good. First class — White Star Lines. Splendid."

"Simply grand."

"Yes, it is best to go in style, isn't it?"

"Oh, I do agree."

"It appears we're losing our sun. Should we move to the terrace?"

"Good idea."

"SWEETHEART, WOULD YOU BE A DARLING AND FOLD THE UMBRELLA? I THINK THERE'S A STORM MOVING IN."

J MURPHY

AMERICA

It's **America.** One mile to New York on a musty and wet 1921 summer morning. My Dad, 18 years old, his eyes and soul tremble as he gazes upon her standing at Ellis Island. He sees the New World. Is that America? He can't look back and he can't look forward. Behind him, he's nearly two months from home. Ahead of him, he's got just enough money for a train ride to West Virginia.

NABEEL HAMDEN

United States of America, 1919.

Upon sinking his life savings into the public offering of the "Deer Brand Beer Company," Bob Loblaw giggled with clairvoyant glee. Dreams would become  reality and prayers would be answered. Dividends alone would be vast enough to retire on. In his mind, he'd be counting dollars forever. But he didn't count on the "Volstead Act." As he sipped lovingly on his last "Deer," the word that was to alter history (at least his) crept through the dark recesses of his mind. PROHIBITION. The empty vessel fell on the train tracks below. So did all his dreams and prayers. The bottle, however, rolled down the embankment, to be found years later by a passerby. It now sits, unassuming and unnoticed, on a shelf in a small restaurant in Round Top, Texas. It was indeed the last call for alcohol.

FIN PATERSON

GIVE ME CONFIDENCE
OR GIVE ME DEATH

Don't tread on me

The Monroe Doctrine

Give me your tired, your poor, your huddled
masses yearning to breathe free . . .

E Pluribus Unum

Give me liberty or give me death

God for the Right

Beat back the Hun

The Nineteenth Amendment

Walk softly and carry a big stick

This land is your land

The Emancipation Proclamation

Remember the Alamo

America's answer: Production

Got a rocket in my pocket

Manifest Destiny

The Model T

Bully!

TRACY SUTTON

"Who you calling **Dummy,** Dummy?"

MIKE MOON

YEAH . . .

Hey! Don't I know you? Yeah, man, it was nineteen seventy-two. May Day Festival in Washington, D.C. Wow, it's been a long, long time. Shades of Crosby, Stills and Nash.

Pulling into a D.C. gas station cum donut shop, six screeching police wagons spoil the mood and change the plan. Later alligator! This city is freaked and amped. Peace and love, man.

Jefferson Airplane, Mitch Ryder and the Detroit Wheels. Dig it! Where did all these people come from? Tents pitched, flags from every state. Going to get our boys out of Nam. Cats in dark suits hiding behind the trees, cameras taking in the whole scene. CIA for sure.

With blankets spread and inhibitions shed, we were movin' and groovin'. Love was in the air. Mind blowing, incense glowing, pass that wine my way.

Hey, what are all those school buses coming here for? Must be at least fifty. My God, they're full of cops! Time to split this scene. Next day news: "Thousands arrested and herded into stadium. Processing will take up to two weeks as order is restored to the nation's capital." You remember that time? Peace and love, brother. It really has been a long, long time.

ARCHIE

PEARSON

SHOULDER TO SHOULDER

Faceless

white markers stare and stand erect, looked on still through stormy eyes on heavy heads. One unassuming piece of stone every six feet for three hundred yards . . . another stone and another, another, another. Smooth dull surfaces that reflect none of the sorrow and regret that follow visitors as they wander by. It is somehow reassuring that they are so regularly placed; as if men stood with arms spread, touching fingertips with the next, planting the remembrances in front of them. Bullets, blood, death and dirge cannot disrupt the formation. A long cool shadow leans into the ragged lawn behind each tribute. The late morning sun lights the front of the grave closest, where 3P.F.C2 is squarely carved into cold granite before the lost defender's name, then 31924-19422. Past this stone, long rows steadily shrink into the distance and multiply so that the outskirts of the cemetery seem solid white rock. Beyond, a huddle of established trees contain the cemetery; respectful oaks and maples drop leaves gently and guard the well-earned peace.

JULIE HEIN

In a striking silk and lace gown, I walked down the
aisle to face the most magnificent man I've ever
met. We were enormously in love, and every ounce
of my being was bursting with happiness so deep
I could scarcely contain my tears of joy. The cathe-
dral was full of family and friends, but in our minds
we were two souls that had already become
entwined. We had soared to our own plane of emotional contentment. We left the well-wishing faces
in our wake as we swirled around the dance floor,
not only until the early hours but into the brilliant
fruitful years that were to ensue.

As the hideous gray face of war settled over the earth, it struck through our happiness and slashed our peaceful existence just as easily as a sword tears its way through the soft skin of a lamb. The faces turned to pallid ash as we lowered all our hopes and dreams deep into the earth. But there is no strength that can shatter our bond — the seeds of love are like steel. In my silk and lace gown, we still swirl to the music on the dance floor in the depths of my heart.

ANGELA ARTHUR

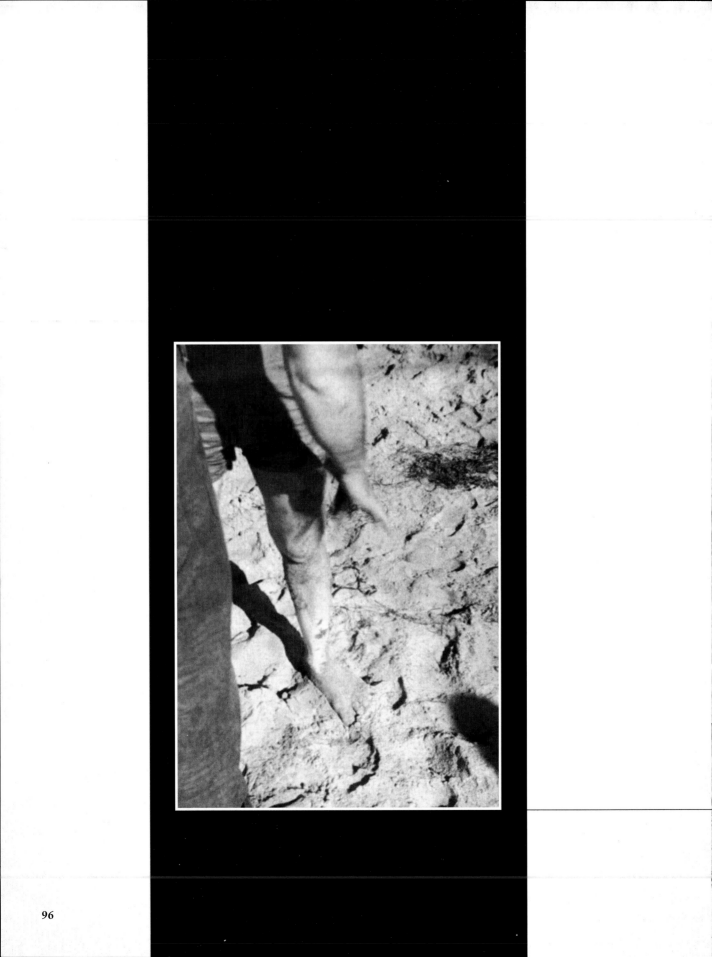

SNAPSHOT

A whispery shiver down your spine. Passionate embrace. An ephemerally

ardent kiss upon your forehead. The salty breeze floats like a gentle mist

breaking on the shore. The rhythmic sway of watery messengers sets you

adrift on the planks of your sea vessel. Warmly floating inside your dream,

a lifetime its making. Watching the sun slide into its nightly hiding place,

a fleeting moment locked into wishful eternity.

BRYAN EISENBERG

THE THEATRE OF THE HEART

The patrons' chatter and laughter competed to overtake the music of a local trio of yet-to-be-discovered country superstars.

My opening line, not exactly Shakespearean, "Can I buy you a drink?" A beautiful leading lady turned, smiled and accepted, her quick glance from my head to toe complete. Her response caused my heart to jump. I was still contending with the knot of summoned courage wedged tightly in my stomach.

She began to ignore the cast of characters that accompanied her. Suddenly, the spotlight shone only on us.

The valued assistance of music, dance and alcohol convinced us that this chance meeting was actually scripted as our destiny. Through slightly slurred speech we mapped out our future together up to and including a "happily ever after" conclusion.

A different setting filled with private passion. (fade to black)

My eyes ached as they adjusted to the harsh house lights of reality. The crumpled program of the night before lay between us.

Our true love story was fiction.

Our performance ended with well-rehearsed lines of future contact. That embrace that still lingers with me to this day.

In the Theatre of the Heart, we're all actors.

BRAD BOECHLER

IT NEVER DID HAPPEN

She was running around the house with her box,
picking up everything that she could lay claim to,
and didn't say a word. There was nothing that
I could do that would make her change her mind.
She was leaving and the only thing I could do was
stare at her cigarette in the ashtray in front of me.
It was like a fuse. As soon as that cigarette burned
itself down to the filter, that door would slam and
she would be out of my life forever. I had exactly
that long until she was gone and all I could think
about was our first day together. I had told her that
someday I'd take her to New Orleans and that we'd
rent out a room right on Bourbon Street. She said
that it would be wonderful but I guess it doesn't
matter now. And then the door slammed and I knew
it was over. I picked up the filter off the table and
threw it in the ashtray.

RYAN KNEBEL

We met in the shade of a cottonwood riverbank. Her sunlit hair the color of campfire embers.

Passion played out in a youthful blush, denial then surrender. An electric touch, glance or impish

smile sparked nights of muffled whispers and sleeping bag caresses. A future reflected in moonlit

eyes. I held her face in candlelit seasons of laughter and tears. We challenged whitewater rapids,

watched the sun rise over ponderosa pine, swam the deep pools, aquamarine beneath granite cliffs,

and weathered the ebb and flow of years of drought and deluge. Now, fishing

the shallow water alone in the gathering dusk, I remember early days and a life overflowing with her.

WALTER KOSCHNITZKE

WITH YOU

MAN GOING THROUGH
REVOLVING DOOR

As far as shoe moguls go, Christopher James Murray was a titan. One man, responsible for selling shoes to the movers and shakers and moms and pops across the land.

Perched in his downtown office, he **baited** shoe peddlers from far and wide to visit with their goods. One by one, they fell to his dangerous tongue.

Christopher always demanded a sharper pencil, and he could not hide his forceful conviction. A shrewd man, he always got what he wanted.

Once tired of the pitch, he'd simply point to the door, signaling that time was up. No handshake was offered.

Leaving the security of his leather-clad office, he would glance from the overhead bridge and watch his victims leave. He would smile as they raced across the marble lobby floor to the safety of the revolving door. The faster they escaped, the more shoes he would buy from them in the future. Christopher liked to be feared. He was in charge.

I am very afraid of Christopher James Murray, for only one reason. I want him to buy my shoes.

JONATHON POLE

REMEMBER

Have you ever dug a hole? You pick up the shovel, and you dig, and you dig. Sweat covers you, your arms feel like Gumby's, and the thought occurs, "There is a whole lot more sand in this little space than I realized." When I think of all the thoughts, demands, tears, baseballs, jokes, ideas, friends, loyalties, books, socks, hopes, attitudes, army men, pain, and dreams I dug out of this room, I wonder how much sand I left behind.

ANTHONY GARCIA

He was most confident in the morning. But now it was after five. Late for the type of business he set out, just after sunrise, to do. And he'd been telling himself since before lunch, "I'm going to talk to the next damn person I pass." He'd passed a hundred or so by now, and that Florida sun was starting to sag low into the horizon. So he proudly remembered his knack for reading strangers and began to press his head for other strengths. And, momentarily, he did recall a handful of triumphs from his past. And this lucidity unearthed a few "good" lines. Most were simple questions, the kind that would make a stranger stop without being the least bit suspicious. All of these lines had earned their keep. Rolling silently over his tongue, they made him feel good.

But this long day of prospecting did have its wear and tear, and he was fidgety, amped up on too many twenty-nine cent coffees. But worst of all, he had been thinking too much.

He stared into the horizon. The Florida sun had dropped. Defeated for the day, it offered him no suggestions. Eyeing his beaten business shoes, he pressed his toe into the hole in the left sole, and surrendered, once again, to more thought.

"The folks over in Gainesville were easy going, laid back. Often eager to give a man a smoke or, even better yet, a roll-away mattress for the night."

He dropped his Top cigarette butt into the sand, not even bothering to mash it out with his good sole. And only then did he know it was time to move on.

Then something caught his eye.

And, his mind began to ease and he patted his six-inch folding Buck knife that hung freely in the reinforced pocket of his Gabardine trousers. His head now clear, he even noticed the cool ocean breeze against his face.

It was near **instinct** that extended his hand in front of him. A secret deep inside him knew that the right handshake at the right time could make or break a deal especially in his offbeat and merciless calling.

"Excuse me sir, I've seem to have lost my car keys in the sand. By chance, could you give me a lift back into town?"

SHANE WEAVER

HONEST!

"All I did was pat him on the shoulder like this . . . honest!"

DOUG NEWMAN

Mary has been gone for seven years now.
She rests, out of breath, on the hill.

I sure do wish that trout would rise.
I know I've matched the fly to the hatch.
Perhaps if I wiggle the line, just a bit.

My youngest child, now married, lives a full day's drive away.
With John's work, I see him but once a year.
And the grandchildren . . .
Well I sure do miss them and with the quickness of time
I'm making do with long-distance kisses . . . Then, the three minutes are up.

I have seen him rise twice, sneer and reject my offer.
If I could outwit the old rascal just once, then back he would go.
I'd catch him again next year, when he's had time to grow.

Little Becky is going on six now.
She's a bundle of energy, full of wonder and wishes.
I want to be there next year when the candles give up the fire.

I've been fishing for this trout for over fifty years now.
Well perhaps not the original, but this is one huge speckled trout.

Tears swell to my eyes when I think that Mary never got to see her.
I guess the Lord needed her a little more than we did down here.
Well, young John sure did well for himself with Cathy.

Must weigh over five pounds. Maybe I'll change the fly.
Yes, perhaps this black gnat will make the difference.

Little Becky looks a little like my **Mary.**
I've mentioned the resemblance, uncanny I think.
Cathy says she can see it from the photo on my nightstand.

It's funny, but sometimes I look into the water and I see Mary's face.
Time is running out . . . the darkness won't falter.
Perhaps I'll give the kids a call.

The paddle blades seem so hollow on the water.
But it doesn't matter . . . there is no haste.
The loon sounds mournful as the ground rises to meet the sun.
Time is now precious and we have none to waste.

WALLY SOLLOWS

He stands in the sea as he explores a new wonder. Thoughts of where it came from, why it landed there and many other mysteries flow in like the waves at his feet, one after another.

Knowing that the sea holds so much to be wondered, exploring for the unfamiliar will be a lifelong experience. Whether washed up by nature or put there by man, the waves of the sea bring continuous life to his imagination.

This **imagination** can take him up and down miles of beach, as every small step makes an imprint on the life and sand the beach holds. Stopping and gathering the waves that softly flow in, he glances out to sea and realizes that what was once so enormous can now become absorbed by the sand beneath his feet.

A young man, full of imagination, at this moment he stands at the edge of both the land and the sea and shares its many wonders.

ART KIOLBASSA

THE ONE IN THE MIDDLE

The **heat** of the day grows oppressive like an anvil crushing your head, like standing in the middle of the Sonoran desert until your eyes feel like the yolk of a fried egg and the legs are day-old wobbly bacon without the sweet early-morning smell you want with your breakfast. The curtains crawl up the wall in an effort to escape the sun's outstretched scraggly fingers — not much of a guard between the oppressor and the oppressed.

Here sitting between boys who don't know when to quit or how to stop fighting, the heat raises tempers like mercury. Tensions raised to tautness then snapping and flying across the workyard like a small stick chopped with an ax that was twenty sizes too big. Sent home for the day, no more work, the quiet after the storm. Both now waiting in anticipation of the release that comes when the one in the middle gets tired. Quietly reading and listening to the day's news while the one is overly dressed with a head being pounded between hammer and anvil while the eyes get fried by the heat of the day encroaching through the window. Who is really being punished, the watcher or the watched?

CHRIS T. DAY

"Don't paint yourself into a corner," mamma always said. She was also fond of "Look before you leap." Did she look before she leaped? Or did she simply walk off that ledge like she was crossing another street? Funny, she was

NEVER UNDERSTAND

wearing that very suit. Her mauve, bordering on taupe, going-somewhere-special suit. The one with the cinched-in waist (mamma never let her figure go, only her mind). When you let your mind wander, you can't always get it back. Was that what she was after when she finally opened up the blinds?

JANE CHAPMAN-KLEIN

SEE

Suicide is **not** painless.

BEV FARR

LOYALTY AND A 7-YEAR-OLD

Sure I arrived just like everyone else: scared, troubled, wearing the face of an adult. Doubt and **misfortune** were the only constants in life. Never really being in one place long. Friends were something other kids had. I didn't need friends. Why should I? They wouldn't be here next year. Even the callous mind of a 7-year-old boy will pass.

It wasn't long before the clan took me in. It's an odd bond when hardship brings children together, not like the love of a brother and sister, but more like a mobster to the mob. Loyalty is something none of us had ever gotten from others, but something we understood. Jenny was the brain of the operation and Curtis, my senior by a year, was the brawn. Timmy and I were about the best two-foot soldiers anyone could ever ask for; we'd do anything for the others. Together we covered the other six like a blanket.

Jenny worked hard on keeping the rest of us in line; being the mother she never had. The only thing we had was each other, and that was fine by me. It was Timmy who heard the news and brought it to the group. From behind the door the information came, adults talking. I was going to be taken away by people in Ohio or Iowa or something like that. Timmy, although you could trust him with your life, has never been the sharpest tool in the shed.

I planned to run away, but I could never leave the family. Loyalty, never read, written or taught, weighed over me. A rule in a world that had none. A heavy hand holding, keeping me put. So I stayed, as long as I could. Often asking Jenny questions about Ohio and Iowa.

Sitting in the car I knew I would never see the Branks orphanage again. . . . In many ways I never left.

CHUCK LICKERT

MAY 1ST

Accompanied by birthday music

She merrily rounds the pole.

Ribbons colorfully dance in the breeze

As her five-year-old hand brushes the hair from her eyes.

Alone, she sits in the silence

Left by the child who was given to another.

Today isn't just any day. It's Katie's birthday.

Sadly she brushes the tears from her eyes.

TINA HAYES

It was for recollection
of a time
swiftly passing.
For remembrance
lest it be overrun
in the waves
of passage and construct.

For each turning point
had a marker.
Some had slipped away
unnoticed
until a chance meeting
or a fleeting *déjà* view.

It was for recollection.
One of many such moments
forming the chain of life,
as strands of pearls
seeking their fascination
gain wholeness and purpose.

The future — welcoming, beckoning
The past — disparate and irrelevant
Now — marking the passage,
the interconnection
A bridge, whose only end
lay in the realm of new beginnings.

And this, a signpost.

HARMONY TENNEY

I remember the day that **photo** was taken.

It was our annual celebration of summer. The sun shone with such force you could feel your skin succumb to its powers. That day the waves rolled on top of each other as if racing to see which one could get to the beach first. This was a day to celebrate.

The cold wet cans of ale were passed around from the cooler. The barbecue was warming up in anticipation of the feast to come. As always, the food created much discussion — what to have, who would do what, the varying degrees of enjoyment and sensation.

On this day it hit me the hardest: I am no longer able to take part in the emotionally charged banter. Of course I smile and make an effort so as to hide the empty pit that is inside me. This day was about everything I was now denied.

I would never taste the salt from the ocean, I would never sample the unique flavour of a seaside breeze. The sweet scent of an overripe banana is lost forever, a ripe cherry doesn't burst into life in my mouth but instead dies a quick and silent death. Food was now merely a means of survival. All enjoyment washed away from me. As I floundered in my sea of self-pity I wondered, could anyone comprehend the sensation of nothing? I vowed to continue to wear my mask and sink my feelings into the depths of my soul.

The bitter flavour of reality is my friends will never taste nothing as I'll never taste anything.

LAURA GELLATLY

Walter's son, his best friend and the neighbor's youngest. Could the big hand climb down the numbers any slower? The seven-day cycle has come around again. A half-hour evening of dented elbows from the tinted polyester shag.

Three sets of eyes prepare to **blink** away the dust of a horse without a guide and two more with leather-braided metal pulling yet pushing their desire to vanish alongside the brother.

The fog behind the glass is ready to disappear with a spark and pop like that of an Eastman going off across the room. The dial borrowed in style from the GE range is set in place. The long arm has almost fallen to the lowest reach possible. When it gets there, the ranching that takes place on the Bahia grass–covered deserts of Johnson Street, severed only by Mother's holler at dusk, will last for thirty more minutes. The only difference will be that the pretending is over and the real thing will ride across the glass.

Walt looks at his watch and slaps his hand to his head. Mom looks at the dial inset on the oven in the wall. The one the boys can see through the wood spindles on the kitchen counter. She shakes her head slowly and knows.

Behind the oven-colored fridge, one hand holding the elbow of the other arm, its hand separating the path between the excited eyes and her mouth, her lips take on the task of passing the words to the father. Words he can see even through his visible eyelids. Trying to decide how to explain the saying, "Spring forward, fall back."

ALLEN HENDRIX

Harry's got five cement squares out front that he keeps like a knight keeps his virgin.

Sweeps 'em once in the mornin', once in the afternoon. More, if those *"got damn birds!"* hit 'em.

Harry's Coast to Coast has been in Brookings since Harry returned in '45.

No one recalls a city council get-together that Harry didn't decorate with grumbles 'bout those *"got damn birds!"*

"Cut dem trees outa da walkway," he says, *"birds'll go den."*

The trees stay. So do the birds.

Most of Harry's customers are leavin' though.

WalMart attacked.

Like the Japs.

And those *"got damn birds!"*

Harry hates the birds — gonna kill 'em all someday. Like how he kilt — before . . .

He didn't hate then — jist doin' his job.

Inside Harry's store ain't so busy no more.

The green hair wearin' the nipple ring can handle things.

But, outside . . .

Harry crouches . . .

Insanely composed . . .

Sneaking . . .

Slowly, steathily, o'er the dung-stained cement.

He's got himself somethin', once and forever, fer dem *"got damn birds!"*

MARK TOLLEFSON

HARRY

BITTER

"I just think that lazy-assed **Rudolph** could help out in the daytime too."

JIM CHAPLAIN

DEAD

Dead is dead. Deader than dead.

You don't feel dead. You feel the opposite of living.

You need dead to know living.

Without dead you don't hear time.

It gets loud sometimes.

Without you knowing,

your applied reality is swept up in a typhoon.

Too late to ask why,

but you recognize you're in transition

from living to dead.

I'm sorry I fell.

You just never know how dead

dead really is.

Until you are dead.

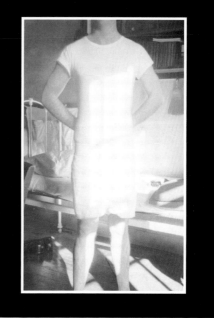

MARK MAURER

131

BAPTISM DAY

I was a news photographer covering Vietnam sent to this naval ship on assignment. I arrived on a Thursday and for two days all the boys talked about was Saturday . . . they couldn't wait for Saturday. "Why?" I asked a young seaman late Friday night. He told me that Saturday was baptism day. "Baptism day?" I asked. All excitement left him as he replied in a slow, solemn voice . . . his eyes blank as if he detached from himself, "Saturday is our day of salvation. The day we cleanse our bloody hands and black souls."

And the caption of my photo read: Cleanse us of our sins. Restore us our innocence.

STEPHANIE MERMAN SLOSS

133

He couldn't sleep that night. He tried every trick he knew, but nothing cured his **insomnia.** So he rose, turned on a light, fished for a pen and paper and began to write:

> *December 6th*
>
> *Dear Mom,*
>
> *Aloha from Hawaii and the USS Utah, my new home!*
>
> *The Utah used to be a battleship, but now they use it for target practice. We spend our days flying around while our flyboys try to drop bombs on our heads. Don't worry, though, they miss most of the time. Even if they do hit us the bombs aren't loaded; they just make big dents! We remain below deck until the bombing stops. Still it feels strange living on a floating target.*
>
> *I miss you all. I hope to see you at Christmas if I can get on a ship headed your way.*
>
> *Love & Kisses,*
> *Your Sailor Son*
>
> *P.S. Here's a picture of me and some of my buddies getting ready for training. Don't we look excited?*

He sealed the envelope, put it under his pillow, and finally went to sleep. Next morning some new flyboys hit their target, this time with real bombs. The letter lies unsent beneath the waves at Pearl Harbor.

MARK HUFFMAN

DEAR MOM

MY GRANDPAS

Robert was born in 1914, married in '35 to "Edie Pearl, the sixth girl" of Reverend Snell of Pleasant View Church of the Brethren. Robert didn't miss a Sunday for over 64 years.

He welded in Fort Wayne for GE in the '40s, missed the action. Good welders were hard to find and needed to build weapons of steel.

Stanley was born in 1911, married to Gertrude Teems in 1936. He spent his wedding night operating the Culver Movie Theater projector while Trudy operated the popcorn and pop downstairs. Jobs were scarce and this was all they had.

He learned telegraphy and became station-master for the Erie Railroad in Servia, Indiana. Uncle Sam told him to stay home to help ship young men and weapons overseas.

Stanley stayed home, dying of boredom in Servia, until he died for real from two-packs-a-day in 1965. His widow missed him, until she joined him in July 2000.

Robert died of welding in January 2000. Wandering to his shop in the bitter cold, he collapsed. He died on January 18th.

It takes all kinds to win a war. Shooters and flyers, diplomats and nurses. And welders and stationmasters — my grandpas.

BRAD JORDAN

"Ding, ding."

Such a sweet sound, that bell.

I gather my bags, waiting to board.

The car rumbles silently down Powell to my stop . . .
the taut cable propelling it along.

With muscles rippling, the gripman brakes . . .
gently, softly, careful not to jar his precious cargo.

Laughter abounds, as cheery tourists dangle precari-
ously, one hand on the rail, appendages outstretched
. . . the classic pose that makes memories.

The car's coat glistens in the midday sun . . .
such breathtaking beauty and irresistible charm.

Hustling, bustling. Every
shape and size . . . every shape of eyes.

I can taste the sea salt air. The wharf's not far,
with its barking sea lions lounging lazily . . .

"Ding, ding."

The moving landmark strikes off once again,
trundling up the incline with ease. Someday I really
should get off and explore this "city by the bay."

JENNY ROBINSON

REMEMBER
SISTER?

Remember Sister? When our summer days assumed the rhythm of the tide.

Soaring on frosty foamy waves we resisted the warmly toasted striped beach towels until at last we burst from the chilly sea. Our brown mother shimmering in contrast to our red bodies, only I inheriting the berry brown of the summer sun.

We'd crunch crispy cucumber sandwiches or the occasional privileged treat plucked hungrily from the red-and-white-striped boxes of fried clams and onion rings. Tastes swirling sensuously with the wind and our own sea-salted fingertips.

When we had soaked in the sea and the sun with the full measure of the tide, we'd retreat to the familiar comfort of the musty house. Hanging our towels on the line coinciding with Grampy's slip into his rhythm of brown whiskey and pungent black cigars. The sweet and loving embrace of Grammy heralding the parade of showers and cool cotton pajamas that signified the moon's pull on the day.

At last we'd be called to take our roost. Bodies radiating perfect joy from under softly worn sheets. Then, once again, the seagull's cry beckoned us to return to the paradise of childhood ebb and flow.

LESLIE BAKER

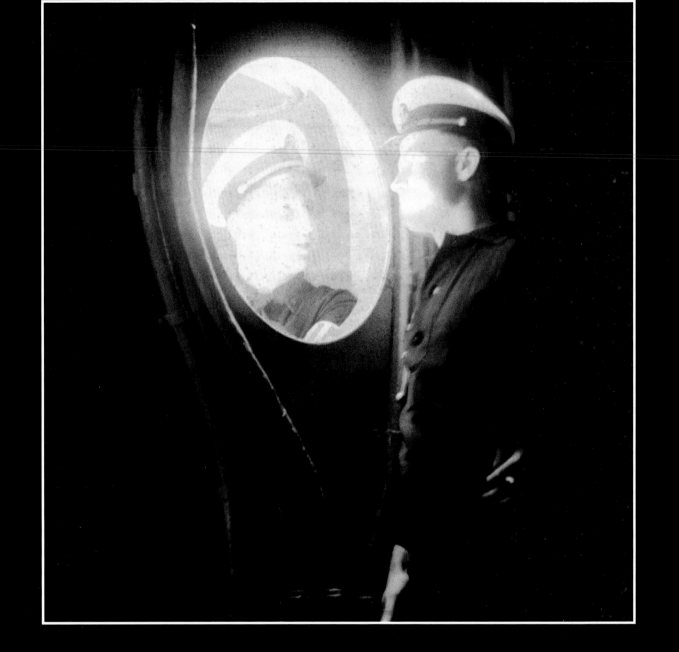

IAN'S LAST IMAGE

It was as if he knew what was coming, that last image captured for eternity as the

illumination entered the cabin. That instant between the light and sound seemed

hours. An instant earlier, the sulfur and oxygen dangerously danced decks below.

Click. An instant later, Ian's camera was hanging from shards of metal, at least my

mind tells me that's what I saw. Flying inverted, thrown into the mystically messag-

ing abyss as the ship shirkedly crackled, my eyes pierced lifetimes of agony. As the

bubbles gave way to atmosphere, entanglement met my foot. Bubbles again

dominated the world. What had me? Was I to survive the blast only to be fluidly in-

graved? As suddenly as it began, the force relinquished its spell, leaving only a small

remnant of its influence. I felt the smoothly rugged leather wrapped round my

ankle. Stars met me as I surfaced to find the camera attached to the strap that was

attached to me. Moments ago, the same camera was poised to capture starry tran-

quility on deck. The only thing sadder that day than Ian's demise was my comrade in

the cabin, 'twas his first eve on vessel. And shaming my heart as I write these last

words, until this day of my life I had never even wondered his name.

VESS BARNES III

143

We were once young sparrows
who ventured north eluding our loving families
When first we flew past
It wasn't known that the universe would have
such frolicking plans
Just enticing enough to draw us there
resting for a moment on that thin branch
only to soar in wayward directions
But fate has nested the unanticipated

Waiting is the branch of another tree

Ruffled and delighted
we recall each other's familiar features
Winds escape quickly
but the branch is anchored
through the days of birth
and the strung lights
time spins a decade

How precious our commitment to this branch
how precious this branch's commitment to us
allowing us to seek and grieve and
linger over tea and rose-printed place settings and
perfumed bottles

Opening our hearts as we fly beyond journeys tasting laughter
and intertwining tapestries
Exchanging creations and noticing glimpses
of each other in ourselves
If anywhere we could feel so free
the world would be much too much
of an extraordinary place
Now, our connected relief is like the North Star
always casting a glimmering ray of welcome

Let's meet again
and always on this sturdy branch
to indulge our spirits
and capture memories of a time when we were
young sparrows
meeting by chance
on a thin sturdy branch

KELLY BRIDGES-STUDER

The ignorant and judgmental, who walk with their noses high, care not for you or I, they say, "Look at him in his shabby clothes. Who cares what he does, where he goes." They say, "Why can't he be like me and sit under the popular tree and drink the good life as it should be?"

But those ignorant and judgmental fools are not as lucky as you or I, for we surely drink of the good life, though not from the popular tree. Our trees' roots run deep in integrity, and drink in the water of love, and not in the beguiling stench of pride.

Now, imagine if I, uninvited, were to sit by their tree. Think of the hate and malice that I would receive. And then being offered to drink of their tree. Would that be very wise of me?

Now, imagine if they were to sit by our tree, think of the love and compassion that they would receive. And they being offered to drink of our tree, it takes no imagination to see that they would still blatantly spurn and leave.

Now, who is wiser? Them, or me?

MICHAEL R. DREW

He, like the tree, more surprisingly me, stood steadfast **silent** when the degree of his thoughts conveyed sucked the horizon away. An anonymous canvas his gift.

RICH CARR

Dear Vivian,

I just got home from the long drive to our fiftieth high school class reunion and found this picture as I was rummaging through some old stuff. There he is again just skinnier and with lots more hair, the center of attention back then at the dance just like he was at the dance just two nights ago. Some things never change! Just look at Peggy Sue, she is leaning on every one of his breaths just as she did the other night, as she almost fell out of her wheelchair. What a hoot!!! And of course there is you and me just looking at the camera just ignoring all that is going on at the other end of the bench. You know we always had fun with him but we sure didn't get caught up with his vanity, even after fifty years. Do you think that means we were mature for our age back then or maybe we just didn't have a clue? Well, time will tell.

Yours truly,
MaDell

BUD ROYER

REMEMBERING ROBBIE

Gene hates this one. Well, really, he hates Robbie.
Although he knows I've really never talked to him
since.

I just can't let go. I still write, although less since
Roberta's wedding. I can pour it out on paper and
at least I feel empty for a while.

It's like he's **afraid** someday I'll hear back
from him.

Letting go. It's the hardest thing. Robbie's probably
the only one that has.

Two days after this, I wake up. Robbie's gone. I send
them to the only address I have: a stupid number on
a black wall.

Poor Gene, I suppose I should just let go, but
I probably won't.

DAVID YOUNG

A cherry ginger ale dawn tickled my eyelashes and tumbled me over the edge of sleep, into the downy clutch of my pillows. A pair of warblers giggled away the last drifting fog of dreams, as Mama's voice danced daylight from behind the Blue Ridge and into the sky. The sun always danced for Mama.

The **aroma** of eggs and bacon chased the fragrances of dew and grass tumbling through my curtains. A percussive counterpoint of skillet-sizzle, wooden spoon click-clack, and breakfast plate–thunking braided itself with birdsong and light into Mama's voice.

Jouncing from my bed to join the kitchen cacophony, I descended the stairs, feet flirting with narrow wooden treads as their chill kiss tickled my toes. A hot pan of biscuits waited under a fresh, red-and-white windowpane-checked cloth. Sunshine flooded the room, the white porcelain of sink and icebox and stove shining like a holy benediction on Mama's labors. And rich as butter on the first bite of biscuit, warm as the light washing in her kitchen window, indelible as the scent of honeysuckle on the breeze, Mama's voice lovingly welcomed me into the glorious morning.

The morning always danced for Mama.

D'ANN CRAFTON-SMITH

HOME
COOKED

LEARNING TO DRIVE

I think we'll go look at that **appaloosa** outside the valley today. Susan needs to practice driving. Hours and hours of driving. I wonder why we never end up doing anything but looking over a corral fence?

See the deer on that ridge? Not you, Susan! Don't take your foot off the gas! You have to keep up your momentum. You'd think he had to get out and push. Keep your eyes on the road. Okay, Dad.

It sure is nice of you kids to take us out for dinner. That's okay. Take the keys, Susan. Okay, Dad. Watch that curve up there. Hey, look at the deer in that field over there. Not you, Susan!

Will this be okay for dinner? Sure. Okay, let's go in. Surprise!!!!

Happy 80th Birthday, Dad.

SUSAN KOEHLER

FRIBBLE AWAY THE DAY

Cheap perfume that teases the young men.

She tries to cheat time and stay that adolescent tomboy.

She loses.

Childhood friends becoming **flirtatious** love interests.

CORRINE TAYLOR

157

CROSSROADS OF
THE PACIFIC

Her last words to me were, "I need some time to see through my thoughts."

I then thought to myself, "Maybe she's right . . . they say time heals all wounds."

I have time . . . but does she? Does she want time? Has her decision been made? Love is strong, but is it stronger than the pain?

She's always dreamed of **seeing** the world, the places that she has only read about. I think to myself. In her way . . . did I stand? Without me, could she have?

From the first moment she received the news, I believe, she decided that Heaven was a better place than to live on earth in pain. I think from Heaven she'll visit all those places that she dreamed of seeing.

RICK FINK

Daddy would often fall and bruise his knees on the sidewalks and the black tarmac and the curbs of our neighbourhood. He would dive and tumble and roll like any other play-mate. From his stomach, he would rise and hurl the disc like an Olympian . . . always to me. If we sprinted across Mrs. Henderson's front lawn, so would he; and he'd defend us when she emerged with her broom and her craggy-old snarl, disarming her with a smile. When Mother called us for dinner he would return like a giant child — sweating and dirty with torn pants. But his shoes were never scuffed . . . he always set them on the porch immediately after work, before he joined us. He'd run back and forth in his stocking feet . . . bruising his heels and stubbing toes, smiling. Mother could always mend his pants but we couldn't afford another pair of leather shoes.

GRAHAM FADER

Billiards was the chosen match last eve down at the old New River Saloon. My jaw,

plaster-posed from laughing, still aches from the joy. Like wolves, we grappled over the

first dance with the blonde gal from Charleston. **Sun-burned**

skies swirled and evolved into the perfect color of summer . . . as the jukebox hummed

the soundtrack that belonged to evenings like that. Night faded into stories we had

heard before, and for some reason we still laughed . . . at least until Jeremiah started

talkin' 'bout his old man. Sleep was the one thing heavier than my thoughts and

I drifted off to peace. Six a.m. . . . like soldiers, we jolted from our ground beds and

attacked the river. Four against the rapids . . . against the world . . . against all the

elements inside us! Armed with rods and reels and God's undeserved protection, we

gentlemen, like redwoods, entwined our roots and rose to battle. Each of us strong,

but together invincible, at least in our minds. Today the river humbled us, but like

drunken dogs, we forget . . . and are soon off with silly grins staggering to the next rush

of insanity. . . . After supper, we hiked to this miracle of a place in our imaginations.

LORAN NICOL

163

Such a look, is it **sin,**
On his grimacing face, full of chagrin, maybe disgrace.
Not smiling, he's wincing, not laughing out loud,
Hopes no one is looking, there isn't a crowd.

It looks like he's leaving,
To get out of town.
He's waiting till dusk
When there's no one around.

His thoughts not so pure,
His purpose not kind.
He's not for the poor, or the lame, or the blind.
But his motives are sound, not a tiny bit rotten,
And when he is gone, he will soon be forgotten.
He's certainly not like the fraidies or shadies,
He just had to go badly, so he went to the "ladies."

ARMAND ARONSON

HE'S GONE

HERE KITTY, KITTY

Bobby Whiffomine **kicked** his cat right in the knee.

Slapped with a 55 in a 35 the big boss Mr. Hartingloot was in a bad way. He screamed to his secretary Mrs. Rankenfuss, "Where's the Hassenfeffer report?!" "Oh I gave it to Pearlputter," she replied. In a threatening tone the boss warned, "Find Pearlputter pronto." Rankenfuss thought to herself, "If it wasn't for me this place would fall apart." "Pearlputter!" she barked. "Where's that Hassenfeffer report?!" "Oh I gave that to Whiffomine." "I need that report yesterday. Find it or it's your butt." Pearlputter turned and muttered to himself, "If it weren't for me, this place would go under." "Whiffomine!" Pearlputter yelled, "HASSENFEFFER!" She had the report all along. "Need it back after lunch, no excuses," said Pearlputter. Mrs. Whiffomine turned in a huff whispering to herself, "If it weren't for me . . . "

That evening Mrs. Whiffomine came home to a messy messy mess, and there on the couch little Bobby Whiffomine with his finger in his ear. "Get that finger out of your ear, pick up this mess and up to bed young man!" Bobby stomped up the steps and there in the hall was the family cat, which he kicked right in the knee . . .

Life would have been much simpler that day if Mr. Hartingloot had come directly over to Bobby's house and kicked the cat himself.

DAVID HARRISON

NO IDEA

You can't **explain** it.

People always say, "I'd have done this," or "Oh well, I'd have done that." They don't know. No idea.

I could give you all the particulars of a certain situation, and you could think about it and make it sound easy. "Oh, I'd just do so and so."

But if you find yourself halfway through some scenario, no idea how it's gonna end, if you'll be alive, what your next step will cause or not cause.

And all at light speed.

The intense boredom and routine replaced by five seconds of almost frozen time that seems to crawl along, as you wonder if you're already gone.

The smell of smoke, sweat, blood, wet mud.

Adrenaline making you clench your fists like solid rocks to keep them from shaking.

Standing, sitting, walking, sleeping, knowing somebody's right now, maybe, aiming at you, to kill you. And still standing, sitting, walking, sleeping.

Add in responsibility for your buddies, loved ones to come home to, responsibilities for orders, duty, being a man, doing the right thing, not caving, not running and hiding, staying alive.

Man, no idea.

You'd have to have lived through it.

JEFF LUKESH

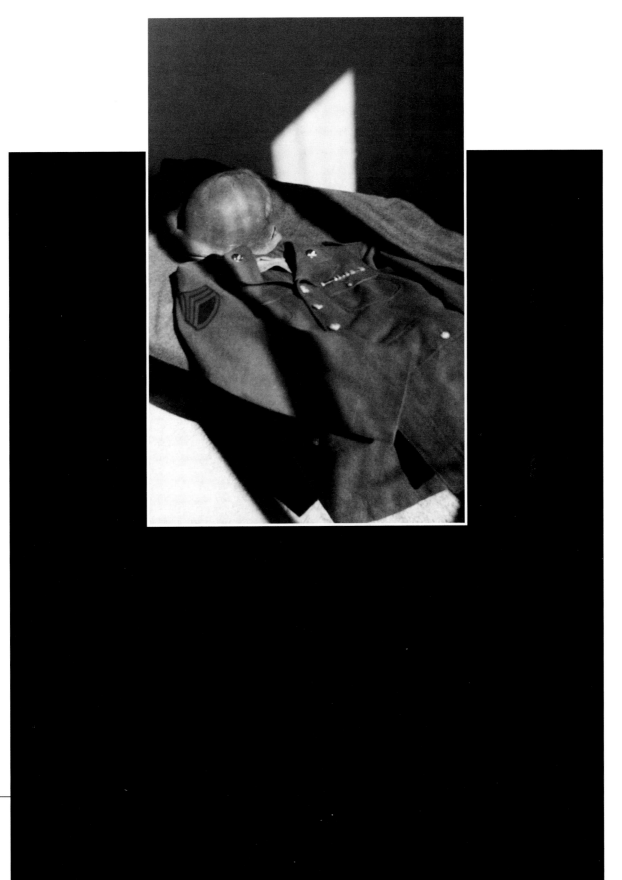

It was so clear that morning. The wind was crisp and salty. The seagulls danced around Bobby and me as if keeping in step with the music emerging into the air. It was Christmas morning, our first date. His mom had worked for this day all year. When his mom laid her eyes on me she knew I was the one for him. After our introduction that day Bobby and I were inseparable. The beach was now ours.

Each year Bobby and I saw the world from our own crude point of view as we went from entertaining ourselves to entertaining others. Starting with friends at quaint gatherings, to the high school talent show, to the local bars after graduation, and finally, our big break on Music Row. Through the fame and lavish attention, Bobby, as always, stayed true to me. There wasn't a show I missed.

The last thing I remember from the storm that night was Bobby's screams fading in the distance as I drifted further and further away. Now as I lie here battered and torn, I have a strange sense of familiar comfort. The wind is crisp and salty. The seagulls dance around me as if welcoming me back home, yet I don't hear the music anymore.

GENA POUNDS

THE
JOURNEY
HOME

Instinctively

peering through delicate lace each time I heard a car. Snow beginning to fall. Finally, there you were, turning onto our street. My heart and I raced, opening the door. I was more giddy than nervous, but you, you were nervous. Fears faded as Daddy firmly shook your hand, welcoming you. Mom beamed, excited that I was in love. Awkward conversation soon gave way to genuine laughter. Outside, the snow gathered quickly. In hours, a thick velvet blanket covered the neighborhood. Driving back to school was impossible. Daddy insisted the sofa was yours that night. Morning found me holding tight to your arm as we walked, breathlessly sharing our plans to move ahead. The air was cold and clean, each step a virgin place. Magical perfection. Never believing I could be more in love than I was at that moment. I was wrong. Forty-three years have passed. I still see our lives as I did that day. Ever forward with excitement, each step cleaving next to you, impressions left behind from where we've been.

WENDY MCNALLY

The sky cradled him in her being, cushioning his dance. Then like a knife ready to slice a steaming piece of sky, he straightened, lengthened, redirected from sky to water. Piercing the surface slightly, it enveloped him, smacking & licking its lips with a quiet contentment after swallowing him whole.

ANDREA OLSON

SLEETING

It's sleeting outside, been a long day at **work.** The weather is angry, the traffic exhausting. Snow falling beautiful, forgetting to stop. Making roads hazardous, wires too heavy. Then lights disappear, and heat stops its warmth. So, putting on blankets, and adding more layers. Time now for sleeping, not getting much rest. Waiting for conclusion, getting no reprieve.

DAWN KNEBEL

Welcome to Continental, our passenger list shows an over-booking, we're seeking volunteers to take the next flight.

Excuse me, Ma'am . . .

Yes

Will you tell me more about volunteering?

Just fill out this form. You may or may not be needed. Thank you for volunteering.

Apprehensive, did I do the right thing? I need confidence. She said I will make it to my destination. I'm approached by a different airline attendant.

This is for you. Thank you for volunteering. We don't need you. Have a great flight.

Okay, I guess. Glad I could help, I guess. I turn and proceed to walk into the plane and keep going until I find my seat. This is amazing. I'm on the plane. Anxiousness mixed with excitement two more emotions to add to this rollercoaster of continuos feelings in this brand new experience. First, look out the window. Oh what a sensation to feel the plane lift off and then to know you're actually in the sky.

I turn my head and see the clouds, I smile. This is my first trip in a plane, and it's special, and I have a window seat.

VALERIE HAMMOND

I knew she was dying. She knew better than any of us but the words for all the

serious stuff of wills and burial plots were simply not open for discussion.

To her each moment was to be lived out loud. Minutes of celebration left now.

If she knew I had this picture, she would visit me from beyond with obnoxious

doings. Perhaps she was the one who opened the cabinet doors this morning.

It is the last picture I have of her life. The cancer had crowded out

all the sane cells. Still, the day before she died she and I were planning to do our

dual face-lift with a big concentration on double chins. We laughed a hearty laugh

but we knew. Death knew too because his smell curved and curled into the

crevices in her room. I miss her. Does she miss me? Does she see me wearing her

hat she gave me for my 45th birthday? Does she know I loved her? I miss her.

KAREN ROYER

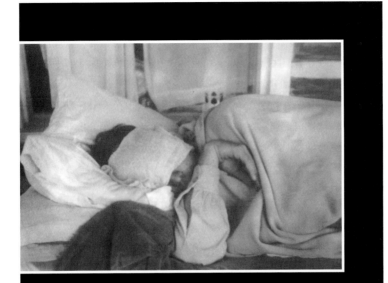

I MISS HER

HE WAS . . .

He was a bastard.

When I look at this picture, I remember what kind of man he really was.

Hard, unbending, demanding, stern.

He smiled seldom and laughed less. He always worked to rise higher . . . personally, professionally . . . whatever it was, it had to be the "very best you can."

He entered the military lying about his age — 17. He never talked about the war. He had Marksman medals, the Bronze Star, and the Purple Heart.

But he never talked about the war.

He completed his college degree with perfect grades. He coached, disciplined, taught — all with that same unswerving drive.

This man . . . this bastard in every sense of the word . . . was my father.

He drove me with the same determination for excellence that he demanded of himself. I was supposed to be a boy. It didn't matter.

He had no father in the 1930s. A bad time to have been a bastard. He died when he was 40. I was 10. I'm thankful. Those years formed my life.

He was a bastard. I'm a doctor.

Love and respect last longer than a lifetime. They last forever.

JUDY JOHNSON

HOME

Butch has swapped his camouflage for industrial blue Dickeys, and he's traded his bootleg Lucky Strikes for a plug of Mail Pouch. His K-rations have been exchanged for Mom's kielbasa, sauerkraut and potatoes, and the trampled sludge of Inchon is transformed into a blanket of snow. Rather than grasping his .45 caliber revolver, he fashions his leathered fingers around the knobby switches of the mill's table saw. The creaky bunk in his old bedroom has replaced his lumpy bedroll, and instead of watching the demise of another **soul,** Butch embraces the season's first yearling.

DAVID F. SALTER

COMPULSORY INHIBITION

A clumsy **swift** kick spins a dusty injured soda pop bottle, circling on a swell of dirt collected beside the street gutter.

He scuttles.

Plippity-skip of a small-tamped stone across the nearby puddle, a rippling skim, the stone is gobbled up.

Arms poised.

In best-leveraged position, a weighty splatter in a brook of liquefying ice trickling from the grumbling faded Coke cooler beside the post office door.

He sits.

Leisurely sifting and funneling parched fine sand through dirty little fingers creating dusty billows of silt in the air.

Thumb engaged.

Pops the head off a charming fair-haired Marigold from the silvery splintered flower box of Mrs. Mabry's store.

He kneels.

Squashing and gluing teeny fleeing ants with sun-softened pale green chewing gum discovered on the curb.

Fist clenched.

Playing conqueror of all evil, waving a sword presented to him by the Red Oak, jabbing the malevolent villain, saving the land from domination.

He rests.

Creating a perfect slow string of spit, bending, arching, in the wind, it triumphs as one thread, all the way to the dirty gritty earth below the boardwalk.

The people shudder, judging, offended, betraying his innocence.

He owns no reticence.

Grow old little boy, go where you will. With confidence.

MICHELLE L. SALZ

"Yikes! I had to pick the only ostrich that could FLY!"

JIM BALLARD

The sun is glistening on your **sun-kissed** face as you flutter through the acres of daisies. As sudden as the sting of a bee, you hear girls giggling and splashing in the lake. Your speed gets faster as your mind jumps with anticipation. Who will you see? With the snap of a twig, the three look up and run for cover. They are looking at you dead in the eyes as you contemplate who is more embarrassed, you or your sister.

When she jumped in naked, she never thought that her big brother would catch her.

BETH C. PLESSNER

SISTER BAY

The flowers of Sister
Bay weave shores of tap-
estry. One is drifting
cold, the other toward
gasping sun. Their tod-
dling yarns dangle from
batts of dark cotton.
They mumble and driz-
zle, tossing words into
alphabets. Woof and
warp, thin and broad.
Lazy petals puddle
amnesia — still cold,
searching still. Perhaps
shadows and wrinkles
will compass and prod,
and boomerang to gold
their memories.
Bayberry flame quietly
sings the song, in a
home that waits for two
friends and a blanket.

STEVE MCKENZIE

MIL VIOLINES

Un cruce de miradas . . . .
Tus párpados se bajan.
Yo insistente te miro
y tus ojos me encuentran.

Resuenan los metales.

Te miro nuevamente.
Tu sonrisa me llama.
Me acerco.
Te aproximas.
Tu voz es mil violines
que suenan en la noche.
Mis dedos tocan piano.

¿Silencio de silencios?

Suena el último arpegio
de mi sonata triste.

Te vas . . . .

Los murmullos de la ciudad
sirven de fondo
a nuestra sinfonía
en soledad mayor.

GUILLERMO S. GARCIA

THE FIRST DIESEL FREIGHTER

I sit on her hatch deck choked in film of diesel. Lines to draw, time to kill and mean progress to be had. Six thousand tons of Duluth's finest red dirt we haul to the blackened factories of hell in South Detroit. We are making Woodies, Crestlines and history on this maiden voyage.

Our Benson Ford at 760 feet is not the grandest of ships on the big lakes, but she is the first to end an era for many. I have sailed these waters for forty years on steamers. Freighters with bellies bursting with fire, majestic head of steam billowing and the bitter embers floating from their stacks will soon be gone.

I wonder if the **sadness** I hold in my heart is that of my brothers gone with the tall ships of wind and sail when first the steamers chugged into port.

We move forward with time and evolution in this supremest of lands. What is to be had of that which was laid to rest in our path? Is all that has sentiment to be lost and mourned? Or celebrated in the wonder of those colleagues past?

Not a moment more of thought be shed on matters as trivial as the navigation of life, not with pistons to oil and tethers to mind. Many of our greatest passings come and go with nothing more than the rising of the sun.

PETER STARKEL

"You've no idea how **bloodthirsty** I've become," wrote William Avery "Billy" Bishop to his fiancée Margaret. Billy was circling enemy territory in his S.E.5 as a fighter looking for his seventeenth kill in just five weeks at the front lines. There was little training provided to new recruits and the average life span of a war pilot was eleven days. Billy was searching the skies for the enemy flying ace Baron Manfred von Richtofen and he had saved most of his 97-round drum of 0.303 bullets for the "Red Baron." His plan was always the same, fight with your back to the sun, gain altitude and circle hard for the kill, then circle and kill again.

BOB TOOGOOD

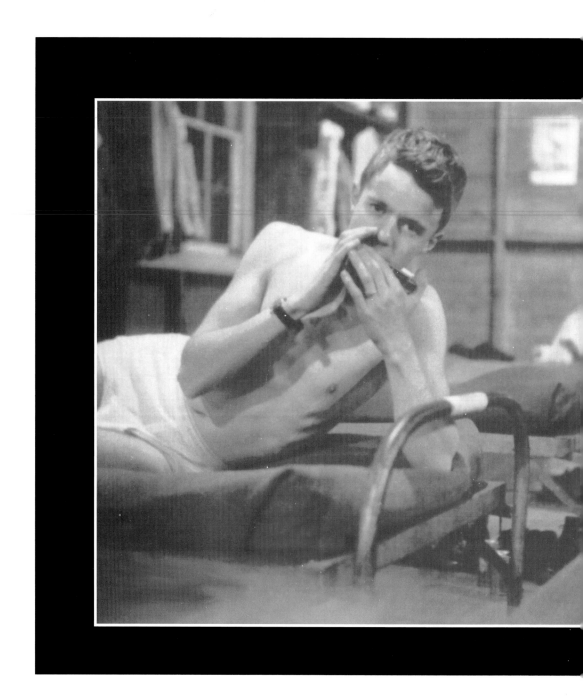

Not Navy. Nothing Royal here. It's a screechy,
wailing Blue that paints fluffy white clouds on a
cold concrete lid.

Raise it to your lips for a **tantalizing**
taste of freedom held inside the wood & metal tool.
Push the pendulum up. Build the tension higher and
higher till every eyebrow arches; then pull it back
down. Slide into a fine walking line.

Torturous to bring the music of movement to a
place so devoid. The train, the delta, the crossroads.

Hang the note out there. Build up the tension.
Shatter the glass. Bend the bars.

GARY SCHERTZER

For weeks I had picked her up every **Thursday** in the alley behind the seed store. Three years, since she was 13 and a half I reckon. I loved her more than a feller with a wife and thirteen chillens should. She was so young when I met her that I could still smell the talcum powder her mum rubbed all over her soft-as-a-pig's-butt skin. Three years and no one had an incklin' that I loved Gertrude. Then one day when it was still lit out, we took a chance we'd never takin before, we went down to the fishin' hole. I was gonna pick some lilacs fer her and she wanted to wash her feet, since she hadn't bathed for a week or so. Well wouldn't ya figure, the man with ink-stained fingers was down there with one of them there Land Cameras er whatever and he took this picture and it ended up in the local rag. This was the last time me and Gertrude were together. Her momma and daddy sent her off to somewhere, they call it a nunnery. Must be where ya don't get nun or somethin'. I ain't had much schoolin' but I even writ a poem for her. . . . Robert Frost it ain't, but preddy good if ya askin'. Here it was:

Gertrude, Gertrude I love ya much,

Yer body I loved to touch.

Good luck wherever you are,

Ya cost me my marriage, and my new gud damn car.

By: Heiko Hartke

JEFF FYLLING

DREAMS

Minnows become whales

Sticks fend off dragons

Boxes form castles

Dreams are like wildflowers

Splashes of crimson, gold and mauve

Young . . . and boundless

Conformity gives birth to a predator

Sweeping across our minds as we age

Like a plague, engulfing all before . . .

With a sad . . . sheet of grey

The herd hide in shoeboxes

For fear of rejection and loss

Faded, torn and wasted

Musty and rank . . . they lie and rot

Rejuvenate your being

Plunge off the path

Crash through the thicket

Throw back the veil of grey

Sunsets are the beginning

The impossible is just a step

Palettes of colour . . .

Our gift at conception

Pierce the sky

With your castle of colour

And shout from the clouds . . .

Minnows . . . become whales

CRAIG ARTHUR

WERE THEIR LEGS TOO LONG OR
THEIR SKIRTS TOO SHORT?

Zelda, Zena and Zowie
were three women with impeccable class.
Then one day lost their heads to fashion
and wore skirts cut up to their —

BARB PATES

I can't figger out why I'm **shakin'** so much. Twelve hours runnin' a jack-hammer ain't for everyone. The pay isn't to my likin' so I give myself a tip at the end of the day. A small nugget or two weighs heavy in my pocket. That's all.

"Come on, kick his ass!"

The boss ain't missed it. Ain't said nothin' to me about it. I been doin' it for three years now. Got quite a stash. Another year or two and call me gone. Flip my tin hat for a spittoon. Hang out with people that don't smell like somethin' just dropped from a tall horse. Drink some real whiskey. Buy some land. Build a nice house. Start a family.

"He's a bum!"

From my rack this is a sure thing. I know it is. I'm lettin' her ride. Get a win today and those extra years of shakin' and tippin' myself don't happen.

"Oh, no! Come on . . . get up! Get up . . . "

JEFF HAUGE

I the King enjoy the vastness of my kingdom. I the King have been graced

with separation from my woes. Sentenced to perpetual happiness I the King

need only look from the window of my cell. With closed eyes, I the King

travel across the flowing hills upon my mare's throne, make love to my

beloved Queen, hold in my grip the sword of my Father

and his Father before him. I am free, I the King, born of royalty I live here in

this tower as King. I thank my captors for taking away my prison and setting

me free.

SERGIO GARCIA

Verbal protests hung low like a ceiling. Like the kind in an old wooden garage, where unfinished projects all swirl together; half-lacquered cabinet doors, piles of tractor parts, soap box derby partially unpacked. Protests here had no authority, and few things are as vexing to a boy as a volley of virulent insults virtually ineffective on a girl. Voices were hoarse from yelling at her. Every time he threw up a shot she would guide it through the hoop, and smiling, would say, "two points." When the others threw up a shot she'd bat it away from the hoop, chiding, "sorry." This kind of abuse ends by calling the game. But something in us found it hard to walk away no matter how demoralizing. Her devotion for the boy she loved splashed onto us like rain pouring off the roof. We were in the presence of a love no one on that court could silence.

When devotion remains undaunted in the face of insult, insult that rages unbroken, insult that is charged with venomous hate, threats, and dirty looks, victory triumphs with a force so great as to utterly silence the opposition. It is then that love breaks into the scene like the eruption of the Kingdom of God. It is now too late to pretend the power meaningless. Nevertheless that is what we did that morning, and most of the next summer. Scarcely a man can know such devotion, such unmitigated godly power. Like the man who, asking the angel's name, discovered it was "too wonderful" to understand. I knew her name though, for it was my feeble shots she guided through the hoop. For me she endured abuse, pouring what little reputation she had onto my feet. It was 48 to 4 before they left. This was not about a game of basketball; it was something bright and lovely like Christmas on my driveway.

ROGER L. BURKE

FOR SALE

What is a dream?

That thought that lights your being with hope

And your spirit with a drive not fleeting nor
wanting of rest?

A dream is a tireless labor

Of hours and days and years and seasons past.

Until one day, with no warning,

Your dream comes no more.

BOB LONOWSKI

101 WAYS PEMMICAN CAN RID
THE WORLD OF BOY BANDS

It comes for me,

Only a taste in the back of my mind.

Sliding past a blink

Scratching away my wide eyes.

Melting a plastic smile.

Stealing pieces when I'm blind.

Taken.

A child led into an alley

Shadows slick over me,

a warm speck in the cold forever.

Sunken thoughts ice into metal rage,

piercing a bent chest.

It festers.

Nurtured in wet purple desires.

The bitter taste of happier times,

burns up from my gut,

leak from this gray soured face.

I'd give anything to drink that perfect day.

On my knees with a limp back.

Just pour it over this rolling head.

I feel sick.

Wallowing

Focusing on the fucked up.

Why was I chosen?

Why did I follow?

Or was I dragged?

It doesn't matter

I'm there

Can you feel me?

Tonguing your broken spine,

Dragging my nails across your rusted soul.

I've come for you.

REX WILLIAMS

I hated my sister when I was a kid. Jennie was older and smarter until one postmortem autumn afternoon. In front of old man Mckinnley's place. Empty since his death. He was found tethered, intelligently arrayed, weathered hat, wing-tipped soul, haunting smile, eyes beaming. This day, the devilish sun was radiating heat like wild cats in passion. As always, the ghost of Mckinnley hung in the air . . . a dark volcanic cloud without conscience or pride. This was my day. You see, I had made peace with Mckinnley. It was in a dream. He was smiling and crying over a life of broken lies and unfulfilled promises. I saw him as the weak man that he was. Jennie did not. And the experience of this day would stir the inner chambers of her infertile mind beyond cognition. The sun shadows cast eerie reflections of a ghost-like Mckinnley. This photo was taken just six days ago. But it wasn't until today that Jennie captured its meaning and the effect it would have on her remaining life. For the man in the photo wasn't really Mckinnley. Tethered, intelligently arrayed, weathered hat, wing-tipped soul, haunting smile, my eyes beamed towards her when she discovered me in front of Mckinnley's place.

ROSS HUGUET

GHOST OF MCKINNLEY

THE WAITING

We wait. Imperceptible
progress taunts us as each
degree of darkness colors the
path. Eluding warmth beckons
with armless colors each equal
to the nth degree. We wait.
How long is unquestioned, still
the answer grasps our backs
with sweet cotton swath.

We wait.

JOHN WHITE

In May of 1953 the Drimildarians of Darius dripped through the sieve of space-time to appear amid the "damn near ripe 'n' ready" oranges of Beauregard LeMeilleur. Beau, having just topped himself up with Mr. Jim's liquid courage, swallowed hard on the itchy taste of awe and fired off two rubbery rounds. The Drimildarians, not amused, simply wrinkled the fabric of reality with a tug and scudded a few eons thence.

However, in their wake, they left a link. A conical conundrum that has left the past century's most pedigreed grey matter puzzled. (Though, of course, the powers that are assert such a thing never was, is, nor ever shall be.) But Beau, God-fearer, non-rod-sparer, he knew. What they left was a stairway to heaven.

BOB BRANDSON

Oldies band, Chinese food, drinks. Dancing. Odd-looking people dancing erratically, each a character.

First set over. Ron introduces us — blatantly, no subtlety. Awkward.

Second set over. Jim comes over to talk to me. General conversation.

Third set over. He spent all his breaks with me. Excitement grows.

As he puts away his equipment, I walk toward him to say good-bye. Without hesitation, I kiss him on the cheek.

Wednesday, 7 p.m. The phone rings. It's him. Exciting!!! He asks me to go out on Saturday night. Good Margaritas. He double dips — no worry about etiquette. Drives me home, I bend over to kiss him on the cheek. Little peck on the mouth.

Sunday, 4 p.m. He calls. We make plans to go out. The night is comfortable, the water beautiful, the environment romantic, peaceful. We sit outside, converse. I feel comfortable, but uncomfortable. Awkward, but not that bad. I am dying for him to kiss me. Stopping, his arm around my waist, he hesitates. I put my arm on his arm. He bends down to kiss me. Mmmmm . . . Magic.

Next **gig:** Quincy, Massachusetts; September 29, 2001; 6:30 p.m.; small church, big hall; you are all invited.

PATRICIA E. GARCIA

221

He **thought** he had it all: an irate SUV that sent mortal cars cowering for kinder roads as it attacked the rink-like mountain pass, the pompous condo leering down the mountain at the snow bunnies romping in their self-induced delight, skis custom-fitted to be extensions of his own feet and prepared to carve into the mountain, flamboyant skiwear that reeked of this year's catalogs and yesterday's greenbacks, a haughty grin, seasoned with disdain, that provided instant access to the front of the lift line, and an air of pretension that wafted after him, providing a barrier between him and those commoners.

As he commenced his conquest of the hill, he did have all their attention.

He lacked only one element; its absence fracturing his façade of arrogance: The Skiing Lesson.

BILL MONTGOMERY

THE LESSON

SURVIVOR

After much thought and consideration, Ben chose a
hammock as his one personal item . . .

Now, he is wondering if he made a mistake.

MIKE WEBB

Dad missed work this day. First time ever. He took us all to the beach. And oh what a day!

Dad did not speak. I know he wanted to. I saw him wet his lips as if to whistle, and he came close to a smile more than once. I think he really was afraid of making any sound at all. Like perhaps just the clearing of his throat would wake an angry god who would quickly flatten a tire or perhaps fill a child's bladder just as we got onto the highway.

I wanted to hear my father speak. I pleaded silently, desperately. Just say the words. Call me by my name.

I remember Mom's soft hand, her ring, each gentle word a precious stone.

This day Dad finally understood that treasure. The luster of all those years of encouraging words.

WHEN DAD FIRST LEARNED TO SPEAK

His lips parted then closed. Then they came. Special words. Spoken slowly, hanging in the air like ripe fruit. Words spoken to each of us, though I tasted only those meant for me.

I think often of mom's patient and gentle words. How they held our lives together.

But I was changed forever when Dad first learned to speak.

ED DUARTE

THE SURE THING

Lucky

Liam McKee, a wandering soul, lived to test fate. He received a boiling tip and he knew he had to take action — The Bet. It was all that he had — Liam waited patiently with anticipation. . . . His horse lost and the weather inside his head quickly turned to thunder. It was time to put the salty gun into his mouth and unlock the door to death . . . BANG! With all of his past sins glaring, Liam lay near the winner's circle cold and dead.

BART TODD

I hadn't visited the cottage in years, though only a two-hour drive from home. I remember waking that Saturday morning, the bittersweet taste of **nostalgia** tickling my palate. I had barely begun considering the day when an eerily familiar voice sneaked into my thoughts, volunteering the idea. I jumped, sending it scuttling back to the buried recess from which it came. It returned, refusing to be dismissed. So I went. I went and I reminisced by the water all day, my tears extinguishing the ultraviolet haze burning at my face. Sometimes I'd turn, convinced that someone was there. Yet I was alone. Alone with my memories. I remained, reliving the fond ones, every single one of them. A sense of calm emerged, cleansing, assuring me it was okay to go. I rose, and in a gesture of affection, I paused, smiled, and took this picture before heading for the car.

It was in that very car two weeks later that I first saw the photos. Though I remembered nothing special, I had been as anxious for their return as a child on Christmas Eve. I thumbed frantically, my hands working on directions of their own. In the middle of the roll, I stopped. Everything stopped. And for the first time since I was a little girl, I was looking into the eyes of my father. And he was smiling back at me.

TOM WALTERS

230

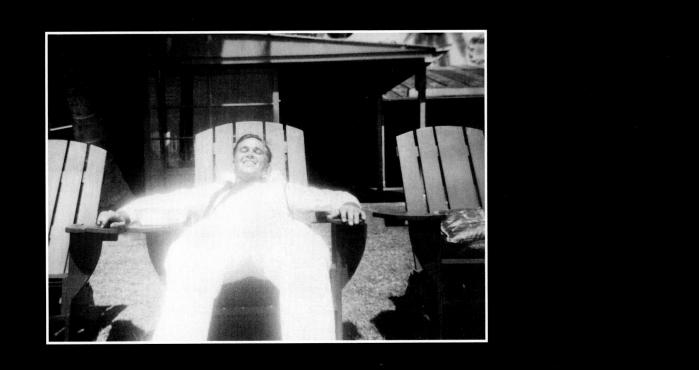

Allen Hendrix
Pensacola, FL
ahendrix@olivebaptist.org

Andrea Olson
Lewisville, TX
andreaolsen@email.com

Andrea Wells Miller
Austin, TX
millerak@quixnet.net

Andy Winnie
Southfield, MI
awinnie@gdrg.com

Angela Arthur
Townsville, Queensland Australia
Aarthur@rgcapitalradio.com.au

Anthony Garcia
Austin, TX
agarcia@kixl.com

Archie Pearson
Buda, TX
archie@wizardofads.com

Armand Aronson
Lowell, MI
armand@joyjoyjoy.com

Art Kiolbassa
San Antonio, TX
artkilo@aol.com

Barb Pates
Fargo, ND
bpates@airfargo.com

Bart Todd
Winnipeg, Manitoba Canada
bart@q94fm.com

Beth C. Plessner
Sioux Falls, SD
beth.plessner@results-radio.com

Bev Farr
Sioux Falls, SD
tfarr@qwest.net

Bill Montomery
Columbus, OH
billm@columbus.rr.com

Bob Brandson
Winnipeg, Manitoba Canada
bbrandson@home.com

Bob Lonowski
Seymour, IN
BBSTORES@aol.com

Bob Toogood
Winnipeg, Manitoba Canada
toogood@q94fm.com

Brad Boechler
Ottawa, Ontario Canada
bradb@chumgroup.com

Brad Jordan
St. Louis, MO
bjordan@jlgroup.com

Bryan Eisenberg
Brooklyn, NY
bryane@futurenowinc.com

Bud Royer
Round Top, TX
bud@royersroundtopcafe.com

Chris T. Day
Denver, CO
chris@tjfr.com

Chuck Lickert
Lockhart, TX
chuck@wizardofads.com

Corrine Taylor
Buda, TX
corrine@wizardofads.com

Craig Arthur
Townsville, Queensland Australia
carthur@townsvilleradio.com.au

D'Ann Crafton-Smith
Norfolk, VA
angelport@hotmail.com

David F. Salter
York, PA
dsalter@ycp.edu

David Harrison
Cartersville, GA
dbma@mindspring.com

David Nevland
Austin, TX
david@wizardofads.com

David Young
Sidney, NE
dsyoung@hamilton.net

Dawn Knebel
Buda, TX
dawn@wizardofads.com

Doug Newman
Kitchner/Waterloo, Ontario Canada
duggyyy@hotmail.com

Ed Duarte
Hamilton, Ontario Canada
duartegroup@sympatico.ca

Emerson "Skip" Robbins
Seattle, WA
emerskip@aol.com

Fin Paterson
Winnipeg, Manitoba Canada
fin@q94fm.com

Gary Schertzer
Ottowa, Ontario Canada
gschertzer@chumgoup.com

Gena Pounds
Austin, TX
gena@wizardofads.com

Graham Fader
Toronto, Ontario Canada
grahamfader@hotmail.com

Guillermo S. Garcia
Quincy, MA
GTASSOCIATES@aol.com

Harmony Tenney
Staunton, VA
Harmony@MyBusinessEmpower
ment.com

Ian Leighton
Prince George, BC Canada
ileighton@telus.net

J Murphy
Sioux Falls, SD
jmurphy@results-radio.com

Jacqui Misener
Stratford, Ontario Canada
mmisener@orc.ca

Jane Chapman-Klein
Etobikoke, Ontario Canada
jklein@capitalc.net

Jeff Fylling
Sioux Falls, SD
jefffylling@hotmail.com

Jeff Hauge
Sioux Falls, SD
jeffhauge9@hotmail.com

Jeff Lukesh
Gurley, NE
jlukesh@crosswalkmail.com

Jenny Robinson
Sauble Beach, Ontario Canada
Rrobinson@bmts.com

Jim Ballard
Austin, TX
Trapdoorhot@hotmail.com

Jim Chaplain
Paragould, AR
jim@bscn.com

Jim Rubart
Woodinville, WA
jlrudini@home.com

John A. Wright
Toronto, Ontario Canada
crash1000@sympatico.ca

John White
Boyertown, PA
jwhite@1075alive.com

Jonathon Pole
Waterloo, Ontario Canada
radiojp@hotmail.com

Juan Guillermo Tornoe
Guatemala City, Guatemala
jgtornoe@yahoo.com

Juan Manuel Garcia
Guatemala City, Guatemala
GTASSOCIATES@aol.com

Judy Johnson
Springfield, MO
jaj329f@smsu.edu

Julie Hein
Cedar Rapids, IA
kziajulie@aol.com

Karen Coletta
Salem, NH
versacchi@worldnet.att.net

Karen Royer
Round Top, TX
dreamer@pointecom.net

Kelly Bridges-Studer
Seattle, WA
kbridges@ackerley.com

Kira Lafond
Racine, WI
kkoo@aol.com

Laura Gellatly
Winnipeg, Manitoba Canada
laura@q94fm.com

Leslie Baker
Dallas, TX
leslieb@Flash.net

Loran Nicol
Stafford, VA
lanicol@pro-image.com

Mandy Barclay
Vancouver, BC Canada
mandy@z95.com

Mark Huffman
Cincinnatti, OH
huffman.me@pg.com

Mark Maurer
Lancaster, PA
golf114@aol.com

Mark Tollefson
Sioux Falls, SD
markideas@home.com

Michael R. Drew
Atlanta, GA
blacklife@yahoo.com

Michelle L. Salz
Rochester, MN
michelle@soldiersfield.com

Mike Moon
Burbank, CA
Michael.Moon@nbc.com

Mike Webb
Springfield, MO
jmwebbadv@oznet.com

Monica Ballard
Austin, TX
monica@wizardofads.com

Nabeel Hamden
Princeton, WV
nabeel@citilink.net

Patricia E. Garcia
Quincy, MA
GTRANSLATE@aol.com

Peter Starkel
Traverse City, MI
peter@starkel.com

Phil Stewart
Kansas City, KS
phil@quick-id.com

Renee Richardson
Sioux Falls, SD
reneer@dtgnet.com

Rex Williams
Austin, TX
rex@wizardofads.com

Rich Carr
Portland, OR
rcarr@RadioWebNetwork.com

Rich Mann
Austin, TX
rich@richmann.com

Rick Fink
Sioux Falls, SD
rickfink@hotmail.com

Rob Seligmann
Galesburg, IL
robs@galesburgradio.com

Roger L. Burke
Lynden, WA
humdinger@NAS.com

Roger Currier
Sioux Falls, SD
roger@results-radio.com

Ross Huguet
Vancouver, BC Canada
ross@greatpipes.com

Ryan Knebel
Austin, TX
NotQuiteB9@New Orleans.com

Scott Broderick
Ottawa, Ontario Canada
sbroderick@thebear.net

Sergio Garcia
Quincy, MA
GTASSOCIATES@aol.com

Shane Weaver
Austin, TX
shane@wizardofads.com

Shelby Reddick Branzanti
Toronto, Ontario Canada
sreddick@rci.rogers.com

Stephanie Merman Sloss
Austin, TX
smsloss@hotmail.com

Steve Coffin
Estes Park, CO
faadvertising@aol.com

Steve McKenzie
Crystal Lake, IL
steve@mckenziemedia.com

Steve Rae
Stratford, Ontario Canada
steverae@cjcsradio.com

Susan Koehler
Rochester, MN
susan@babcockswine.com

Tina Hayes
Boerne, TX
seyah@gvtc.com

Tom Mogush
Marquette, MI
tom@wmqt.com

Tom Walters
Austin, TX
tom@wizardofads.com

Tracy Sutton
Buda, TX
tracy@wizardofads.com

Valerie Hammond
Laconia, NH
staff@wezs.com

Vess Barnes III
Amarillo, TX
v3global@arn.net

Wally Sollows
Hamilton, Ontario Canada
wsollows@cgocable.net

Walter Koschnitzke
Kenosha, WI
wwk53@hotmail.com

Wendy McNally
Fredricksburg, VA
wen@thatbaldguy.com

Located at the northern end of the Central American isthmus, Guatemala is remarkably diverse in climate and terrain. Majestic mountains and volcanoes, breathtaking mountain lakes, tropical jungles, Caribbean and Pacific coasts and the legendary palaces and temples of the Maya adorn this dazzling and colorful country.

But Guatemala needs our help as it struggles to recover from a 36-year-old civil war that left 150,000 people dead and 50,000 missing. Evidence of hostility still exists: armed guards patrol streets and businesses with semi-automatic rifles, human rights violations and kidnappings are common newsmakers and corruption has become so rampant that basics such as health and education are virtually nonexistent. The once proud nation was further thrashed by Hurricane Mitch in 1998, whose effects on agriculture were disastrous.

Students from Wizard Academy have decided to provide personal assistance to the people of Guatemala. One hundred percent of the royalties from this book will also be donated. These contributions will provide help to Guatemala through the Antigua NGO (non-government organization), under the control of Eduardo Prado through El Consejo de Audencia de la Antigua, Guatemala. Here, the money will be managed by Don Roy H. Williams, Don Steve Rae and Don Juan Guillermo Tornoe, according to the advice of El Comendador.

Contributions to Guatemala *(Currently in Progress)*

INFRASTRUCTURE

Bill Bergh
Bringing the Intermittently Operated Slow Sand Filtration (IOSSF) to Guatemala in order to improve suitability of water for human consumption.

Steve Rae
Helping build a school extension in Huehuetenango.

Sheila Lucas
Coordinating people interested in selling or leasing used heavy machinery to be used in projects initiated by the Consejo de Audiencia.

Chris Day
Seeking a company to develop ecologically friendly housing at low cost.

HEALTH

John and Michelle White
Providing wheelchairs and other medical equipment and coordinating doctors and dentists to come to Guatemala to give medical attention to those in need.

Sheila Lucas
Assisting the "Life Project" funding for children's cancer medications through the Georgia Academy of Independent Pharmacists.

Entire Class of Guatemalan Wizard Academy
Contributed money to buy orthopedic apparatus for a handicapped Guatemalan child.

EDUCATION AND AWARENESS

Dana Cooper
Inspired the University of Arizona to become a sister school to a major university in Guatemala. Also, planning to increase awareness of county's culture by bringing Guatemalan musical and theatrical acts to the fine arts department at U of A.

Craig Arthur
Inspired James Cook University (Australia) to become a sister school to a major Guatemalan university.

Steve Rae
Collecting used computers to send to Guatemalan schools.

Scott Broderick
Proposing Antigua, Guatemala as the focus of a large project at an elementary school in Manitoba.

LOCAL PRODUCT EXPORT

Steve Rae/Bill Bergh/Dana Cooper
Working to increase global consumption of Guatemalan coffees.

DONATIONS AND PARTNERSHIPS

John and Michelle White
Organizing a mission trip to Guatemala in 2002.

Scott Broderick
Working with Boy Scouts of Canada toward organizing a trip to Guatemala, where the Scouts would help build homes for the poor.

ADVERTISING

Dana Cooper/Scott Broderick/ Mick Torbay/Steve Rae
Creating a public service campaign to inspire public awareness for the plight of Guatemala.

Chris Day
Invited El Comendador Eduardo Prado to attend Hispanic Media 100 Awards in Miami and gave him free advertising in all event publications as well as in a TJFR newsletter.

TOURISM

Angela Arthur
Proposing an Australian TV travel program to do a segment on Guatemala.

PROFIT

Rich Mann
Encouraging the distribution of electric vehicles and energy storage systems for which a percentage of the profits would go to the Comendador's work.

Chris Day
Encouraging La Fuente Imports, an outlet for Latin American crafts in Colorado Springs, to distribute Guatemalan items. A percentage of the profits will go into helping the Comendador's work in Guatemala.

John and Michelle White
Developing a distribution system of Guatemalan products with 10,000 Villages, a chain of retail shops owned by the Mennonite Central Committe (MCC). Find out more at www.tenthousandvillages.org

ADDITIONAL THANKS TO . . .

Habitat for Humanity
www.habitat.org

Mercy Corps International
www.mercycorps.org

Food for the Poor
www.foodforthepoor.com

Cedar Meadow Farms
www.cedarmeadowfarm.com

Joni and Friends
www.joniandfriends.org

Special thanks to John and Michelle White.

Promising to dramatically improve communication skills, Wizard Academy is a three-day retreat held just south of Austin, Texas. Students are introduced to a variety of innovative communication techniques inspired by legends like Claude Monet, Robert Frank, Ernest Hemingway, and Steven Spielberg. Only a very small number of students are accepted each month. If you're interested in mastering the techniques described in this book, log onto www.wizardacademy.com and find out how you can become a Wizard Academy graduate, participate in *Accidental Magic II*, and help the people of Guatemala.